vegetarian

HOMESTYLE

vegetarian

bay books

contents

The healthy alternative

Far from being any fringe, hippie fad that started somewhere around the 1960s, as some might think, vegetarianism has been with us for a very long time—in fact, Plato and Pythagoras, both famous ancient Greek philosophers, spurned meat.

Some people choose to follow a meat-free diet for reasons of conscience, religion or health. The health conscious amongst us knows very well that the vegetarian diet helps keep body weight under control and substantially reduces the risk of heart disease, cancer and other fatal diseases. For others, eating vegetarian meals, at least a few times a week, is an excellent way to decrease meat intake, which is very wise given how easy it is to overindulge.

Whatever the reason for being a partial, or full-time vegetarian, there is no doubt that vegetarian food ranks among some of the most varied and mouthwatering imaginable. Who needs bacon when there's corn and polenta pancakes with tomato salsa, or egg and vegetable tortillas on offer for breakfast? Lunchtime salad never tasted so good as spicy lentil, or chickpea and roast vegetable, or lemon, fennel and rocket combinations. Stir-fries, risotto, a bake or a stew make for scrumptious mid-week meals that everyone will love when they're flavoured with all the good things of the earth. Plan a dinner party or a special family meal around vegetarian recipes and you'll be amazed at the delicious diversity that's possible. Many of the world's great culinary cultures have strong vegetarian traditions so you can give a spread an Indian theme, a Mediterranean one or even go completely Japanese. Dining vegetarian can lead you down exciting paths toward ingredients like tofu, tamari and tempeh, that are perhaps new to some. Or, it can comfort with the soothing familiarity of pasta, curries, soufflés and moussaka, all boosted with the extra goodness of fresh, seasonal vegetables.

Whatever the occasion and whichever of the innovative, healthy recipes in this book you decide to cook, *Homestyle Vegetarian* will become an essential source of inspiration for all who love to feast the vegetarian way.

Breakfast and brunch

Egg and vegetable tortillas

PREPARATION TIME: 1 HOUR 30 MINUTES | TOTAL COOKING TIME: 1 HOUR | SERVES 4–6

1 tablespoon extra virgin olive oil
2 red onions, finely sliced
1 garlic clove, crushed
90 g (3¼ oz) English spinach, roughly chopped
2 red capsicums (peppers)
1 kg (2 lb 4 oz) potatoes, cut into shoestring chips
vegetable oil, for deep-frying
6 eggs, beaten
3 tablespoons of combined chopped herbs (basil, parsley, oregano)

NUTRITION PER SERVE (6)
Protein 15 g; Fat 20 g; Carbohydrate 25 g; Dietary Fibre 5 g; Cholesterol 180 mg; 1350 kJ (325 Cal)

1 Heat the oil in a heavy–based frying pan and stir the onions over high heat for 2–3 minutes. Reduce the heat and cook for 30–40 minutes, until the onion starts to caramelise and break down. Increase the heat slightly, add the garlic and stir for 1 minute. Add the spinach, toss through and cook for another minute.

2 Cut the capsicums into quarters and remove the seeds and membrane. Grill (broil), skin side up, until the skin is blackened and blistered. Cover with a damp tea towel (dish towel) until cooled. Peel and slice the flesh into fine strips.

3 Heat the oil to 160°C/315°F, or until a cube of bread dropped into the oil browns in 30 seconds. Deep-fry the chips until cooked but not brown. Remove and drain on paper towels. In a bowl, mix the onion, garlic, spinach, capsicum and chips.

4 Combine the eggs and herbs, add to the vegetables and toss through. Lightly grease a small 20 cm (8 inch) frying pan and add enough of the tortilla mixture to cover the base of the pan. Cook over medium heat for 2–3 minutes, or until the underside is golden. Flip and cook the other side. Keep warm while cooking the remaining tortilla mixture.

Cook the onion over low heat, very slowly so that it caramelises.

Cut the capsicums into quarters and grill until blackened and blistered.

Cook the tortilla until the underside is golden, then flip over.

Fruit salad in vanilla, ginger and lemongrass syrup

PREPARATION TIME: 20 MINUTES + CHILLING TIME | TOTAL COOKING TIME: 15 MINUTES | SERVES 4

500 g (1 lb 2 oz) watermelon, cubed
260 g (9¼ oz) honeydew melon, cubed
½ small pineapple, chopped
1 mango, diced
250 g (9 oz) strawberries, halved
1 handful small mint sprigs, plus extra leaves, to garnish

LEMONGRASS SYRUP
125 ml (4 fl oz/½ cup) lime juice
45 g (1½ oz/¼ cup) soft brown sugar
1 stem lemongrass, finely sliced
2 tablespoons grated fresh ginger
1 vanilla bean, split

1 Place the fruit and mint in a bowl and mix gently.

2 To make the syrup, place the lime juice, sugar and 125 ml (4 fl oz/½ cup) water in a small saucepan and stir over low heat until the sugar dissolves, then add the lemongrass, ginger and vanilla bean. Bring to the boil, reduce the heat and simmer for 10 minutes, or until reduced and slightly thickened. Remove the vanilla bean, pour the syrup over the fruit and refrigerate until cold. Serve garnished with mint leaves.

NOTE: *If you prefer your syrup without the lemongrass pieces but like the flavour, bruise the white part of the lemongrass with a rolling pin, place in the syrup, cook and remove along with the vanilla bean.*

Remove the skin from the mango and cut the flesh into small cubes.

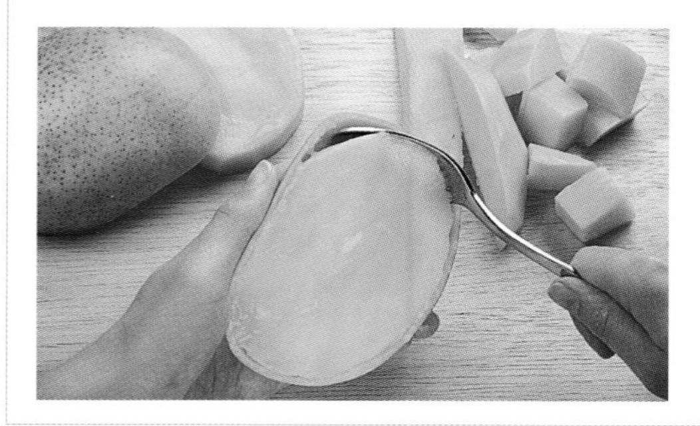

Simmer the lemongrass syrup until it is reduced and slightly thickened.

NUTRITION PER SERVE
Protein 3.5 g; Fat 0.5 g; Carbohydrate 40 g; Dietary Fibre 6 g; Cholesterol 0 mg; 797 kJ (190 Cal)

Fried tomatoes with marinated haloumi

PREPARATION TIME: 15 MINUTES + OVERNIGHT MARINATING | TOTAL COOKING TIME: 10 MINUTES | SERVES 4

400 g (14 oz) haloumi cheese, cut into eight 1 cm (½ inch) slices
250 g (9 oz) cherry tomatoes, halved
250 g (9 oz) teardrop tomatoes, halved
1 garlic clove, crushed
2 tablespoons lemon juice
1 tablespoon balsamic vinegar
2 teaspoons lemon thyme, plus small sprig, to garnish
3 tablespoons extra virgin olive oil
2 tablespoons olive oil
1 small loaf wholegrain bread, cut into 8 thick slices

1 Place the haloumi and tomatoes in a non-metallic dish. Whisk together the garlic, lemon juice, balsamic vinegar, lemon thyme and extra virgin olive oil in a bowl and pour over the haloumi and tomatoes. Cover and marinate for 3 hours or overnight. Drain well, reserving the marinade.

2 Heat the olive oil in a large frying pan. Add the haloumi and cook in batches over medium heat for 1 minute each side, or until golden brown. Transfer to a plate and keep warm. Add the tomatoes and cook over medium heat for 5 minutes, or until their skins begin to burst. Transfer to a plate and keep warm.

3 Toast the bread until it is golden brown. Serve the fried haloumi on top of the toasted bread, piled high with the tomatoes and drizzled with the reserved marinade. Best served immediately, garnished with lemon thyme sprig.

Pour the marinade over the haloumi and the tomatoes and leave for 3 hours or overnight.

Cook the haloumi in batches until it is golden brown on both sides.

NUTRITION PER SERVE
Protein 30 g; Fat 40 g; Carbohydrate 34 g; Dietary Fibre 7 g; Cholesterol 53 mg; 2690 kJ (645 Cal)

Mushrooms in brioche

PREPARATION TIME: 15 MINUTES | TOTAL COOKING TIME: 20 MINUTES | SERVES 6

750 g (1 lb 10 oz) mixed mushrooms (Swiss brown, shiitake, button, field, oyster)
75 g (2½ oz) butter
4 spring onions (scallions), chopped
2 garlic cloves, crushed
125 ml (4 fl oz/½ cup) dry white wine
300 ml (10½ fl oz) pouring (whipping) cream
2 tablespoons chopped thyme
6 small brioche (see NOTE)

NUTRITION PER SERVE
Protein 7.5 g; Fat 33 g; Carbohydrate 15 g; Dietary Fibre 4 g; Cholesterol 100 mg; 1587 kJ (380 Cal)

1 Preheat the oven to 180°C (350°F/Gas 4). Wipe the mixed mushrooms with a clean damp cloth to remove any dirt. Cut the larger mushrooms into thick slices but leave the smaller ones whole.

2 Heat the butter in a large frying pan over medium heat. Add the spring onion and garlic and cook for 2 minutes. Increase the heat, add the mushrooms and cook, stirring frequently, for 5 minutes, or until the mushrooms are soft and all the liquid has evaporated. Pour in the wine and boil for 2 minutes to reduce slightly.

3 Stir in the cream and boil for a further 5 minutes to reduce and slightly thicken the sauce. Season to taste with salt and freshly ground black pepper. Stir in the thyme and set aside for 5 minutes.

4 Slice the top off the brioche and, using your fingers, pull out a quarter of the bread. Place the brioche and their tops on a baking tray and warm in the oven for 5 minutes.

5 Place each brioche on an individual serving plate. Spoon the mushroom sauce into each brioche, allowing it to spill over one side. Replace the top, if desired, and serve warm.

NOTE: *You can use bread rolls, but the flavour won't be as good.*

Cut the large mushrooms into thick slices, but leave the smaller ones whole.

Cook the mushrooms, stirring frequently, until they are soft.

Slice off the top of each brioche and pull out a quarter of the bread.

Corn and polenta pancakes with tomato salsa

PREPARATION TIME: 15 MINUTES | TOTAL COOKING TIME: 10 MINUTES | SERVES 4

TOMATO SALSA
2 ripe tomatoes
150 g (5½ oz/1 cup) frozen broad (fava) beans
2 tablespoons chopped basil
1 small Lebanese (short) cucumber, diced
2 small garlic cloves, crushed
1½ tablespoons balsamic vinegar
1 tablespoon extra virgin olive oil

CORN AND POLENTA PANCAKES
90 g (3¼ oz/¾ cup) self-raising flour
110 g (3¾ oz/¾ cup) fine polenta
250 ml (9 fl oz/1 cup) milk
310 g (11 oz) tin corn kernels, drained
olive oil, for frying

1 To make the salsa, score a cross in the base of each tomato, then place in a bowl of boiling water for 30 seconds. Then plunge into cold water and peel the skin away from the cross. Dice. Pour boiling water over the broad beans and leave for 2–3 minutes. Drain and rinse under cold water. Remove the skins. Put the beans in a bowl and stir in the tomato, basil, cucumber, garlic, vinegar and extra virgin olive oil.

2 To make the pancakes, sift the flour into a bowl and stir in the polenta. Add the milk and corn and stir until just combined, adding more milk if the batter is too dry. Season.

3 Heat the oil in a large frying pan and spoon 2 heaped tablespoons of the batter into the pan, making four 9 cm (3½ inch) pancakes. Cook for 2 minutes on each side, or until golden and cooked through. Repeat with the remaining batter, adding more oil if necessary. Drain well and serve with the salsa.

After blanching, it will be easy to peel the skin off the broad beans.

Cook the pancakes for 2 minutes on each side, or until golden and cooked through.

NUTRITION PER SERVE
Protein 11 g; Fat 18.5 g; Carbohydrate 56 g; Dietary Fibre 8.5 g; Cholesterol 8.5 mg; 1809 kJ (432 Cal)

Mixed berry couscous

PREPARATION TIME: 15 MINUTES + 5 MINUTES SOAKING | TOTAL COOKING TIME: 5 MINUTES | SERVES 4

185 g (6½ oz/1 cup) instant couscous
500 ml (17 fl oz/2 cups) apple and cranberry juice
1 cinnamon stick
2 teaspoons orange zest
250 g (9 oz) raspberries
250 g (9 oz) blueberries
250 g (9 oz) strawberries, halved
200 g (7 oz) Greek yoghurt
2 tablespoons golden syrup
mint leaves, to garnish

1 Place the couscous in a bowl. Pour the apple and cranberry juice into a saucepan and add the cinnamon stick. Cover and bring to the boil, then remove from the heat and pour over the couscous. Cover the couscous with plastic wrap and leave for about 5 minutes, or until all the liquid has been absorbed. Remove the cinnamon stick from the bowl.

2 Separate the grains of couscous with a fork, then gently fold in the orange zest and most of the raspberries, blueberries and strawberries. Spoon the couscous mixture into four serving bowls and sprinkle with the remaining berries. Serve with a generous dollop of the yoghurt, then drizzle with the golden syrup. Garnish with fresh mint leaves and serve immediately.

NUTRITION PER SERVE
Protein 8.5 g; Fat 3 g; Carbohydrate 70 g; Dietary Fibre 7 g; Cholesterol 8 mg; 1448 kJ (345 Cal)

Pour the hot apple and cranberry juice over the instant couscous.

Separate the grains of couscous with a fork to ensure they are fluffy.

Gently fold in the orange zest and most of the raspberries, blueberries and strawberries.

Poached eggs with yoghurt dressing and spinach

PREPARATION TIME: 10 MINUTES | TOTAL COOKING TIME: 15 MINUTES | SERVES 4

DRESSING
125 g (4½ oz/½ cup) sheep's milk yoghurt
1 small garlic clove, crushed
1 tablespoon chives, snipped

300 g (10½ oz) baby English spinach leaves
30 g (1 oz) butter, chopped
herbed salt
4 tomatoes, halved
1 tablespoon white vinegar
8 eggs
1 loaf light rye bread, cut into
8 thick slices

NUTRITION PER SERVE
Protein 25 g; Fat 20 g; Carbohydrate 45 g; Dietary Fibre 7.5 g; Cholesterol 384 mg; 1895 kJ (453 Cal)

1 To make the dressing, mix together the yoghurt, garlic and chives.

2 Wash the spinach and place it in a large saucepan with just the little water that is left clinging to the leaves. Cover the pan and cook over low heat for 3–4 minutes, or until the spinach has wilted. Add the butter. Season with the herbed salt. Set aside and keep warm. Cook the tomatoes under a hot grill (broiler) for 3–5 minutes.

3 Fill a frying pan three-quarters full with cold water. Add the vinegar and some salt to stop the egg whites spreading. Bring to a gentle simmer. Gently break an egg into a small bowl, then carefully slide it into the water. Reduce the heat so that the water barely moves. Cook for 1–2 minutes, or until the egg is just set. Remove carefully with a spatula. Drain. Repeat, one by one, with the remaining 7 eggs.

4 Toast the bread. Top each slice of toast with spinach, 2 eggs and some dressing. Serve with tomato halves and season with cracked black pepper and sea salt.

Cook the spinach leaves until they are wilted, then stir in the butter.

Cook the eggs until they are just set, then remove with a spatula.

Baked ricotta with preserved lemon and tomatoes

PREPARATION TIME: 15 MINUTES + 10 MINUTES STANDING | TOTAL COOKING TIME: 30 MINUTES | SERVES 8–10

- 2 kg (4 lb 8 oz) round ricotta cheese
- olive oil
- 2 garlic cloves, crushed
- 1 preserved lemon, rinsed, pith and flesh removed, cut into thin strips
- 150 g (5½ oz) semi-dried (sun-blushed) tomatoes, roughly chopped
- 2 large handfuls finely chopped flat-leaf (Italian) parsley
- 2 large handfuls chopped coriander (cilantro) leaves
- 4 tablespoons extra virgin olive oil
- 3 tablespoons lemon juice

1 Preheat the oven to 250°C (500°F/Gas 9). Place the ricotta on a baking tray lined with baking paper, brush lightly with the olive oil and bake for 20–30 minutes, or until golden brown. Leave for 10 minutes then, using a spatula, transfer to a large platter. (If possible, have someone help you move the ricotta.)

2 Meanwhile, place the garlic, preserved lemon, semi-dried tomato, parsley, coriander, oil and lemon juice in a bowl and mix together well.

3 Spoon the dressing over the baked ricotta and serve with crusty bread. Delicious hot or cold.

NUTRITION PER SERVE (10)
Protein 20 g; Fat 30 g; Carbohydrate 3 g; Dietary Fibre 0.5 g; Cholesterol 95 mg; 1542 kJ (368 Cal)

Put all the dressing ingredients in a bowl and mix together thoroughly.

Warm asparagus and egg salad with hollandaise

PREPARATION TIME: 5 MINUTES | TOTAL COOKING TIME: 15 MINUTES | SERVES 4

HOLLANDAISE SAUCE
175 g (6 oz) butter
4 egg yolks
1 tablespoon lemon juice

4 eggs, at room temperature
310 g (11 oz) asparagus spears, trimmed
parmesan cheese shavings, to serve

1 To make the hollandaise, melt the butter in a small saucepan and skim off any froth. Remove from the heat and cool. Mix the egg yolks and 2 tablespoons water in another small saucepan for 30 seconds, or until pale and foamy. Place the saucepan over very low heat and whisk for 2–3 minutes, or until thick and foamy—do not overheat or it will scramble. Remove from the heat. Gradually add the butter, whisking well after each addition (avoid using the whey at the bottom). Stir in the lemon juice and season. If the sauce is runny, return to the heat and whisk until thick—do not scramble.

2 Place the eggs in a saucepan half filled with water. Bring to the boil and cook for 6–7 minutes, stirring occasionally to centre the yolks. Drain and cover with cold water until cooled a little, then peel off the shells.

3 Plunge the asparagus into a large saucepan of boiling water and cook for 3 minutes, or until just tender. Drain and pat dry. Divide among four plates. Spoon on the hollandaise. Cut the eggs in half and arrange two halves on each plate. Sprinkle with parmesan shavings to serve.

NUTRITION PER SERVE
Protein 20 g; Fat 35 g; Carbohydrate 15 g; Dietary Fibre 1 g; Cholesterol 605 mg; 1935 kJ (460 Cal)

Gradually add the cooled butter, whisking well after each addition.

Cook the asparagus in a large saucepan of boiling water until just tender.

Corn muffins

PREPARATION TIME: 20 MINUTES | TOTAL COOKING TIME: 25 MINUTES | MAKES 12

310 g (11 oz/2½ cups) self-raising flour
75 g (2½ oz/½ cup) cornmeal
250 ml (9 fl oz/1 cup) milk
125 g (4½ oz) butter, melted
2 eggs, lightly beaten
130 g (4½ oz) tin corn kernels, drained
2 spring onions (scallions), finely chopped
60 g (2¼ oz) grated cheddar cheese
butter or cream cheese, to serve

NUTRITION PER MUFFIN
Protein 6 g; Fat 12 g; Carbohydrate 27 g; Dietary Fibre 1.5 g; Cholesterol 65 mg; 1009 kJ (240 Cal)

1 Preheat the oven to 210°C (415°F/Gas 6–7). Grease two trays of six 125 ml (4 fl oz/½ cup) muffin holes with butter. Sift the flour and cornmeal into a large bowl and make a well in the centre.

2 Whisk together the milk, butter, eggs, corn, spring onion, cheddar and salt and pepper in a separate bowl and pour into the well in the flour and cornmeal. Fold gently with a metal spoon until all the ingredients are just combined. Do not overmix—the mixture should still be very lumpy.

3 Spoon the mixture into the muffin tin and bake for 20–25 minutes, or until lightly golden. Leave for 5 minutes before removing from the tin. To serve the muffins, split them in half and spread with butter or cream cheese. Delicious either hot or at room temperature.

VARIATION: *Muffins are so versatile, you can virtually add whatever you have in the cupboard. Try adding; 2 tablespoons snipped chives, 40 g (1½ oz/¼ cup) chopped, drained sun-dried tomatoes or capsicum (pepper) in oil, 2 finely chopped red chillies or ½ finely chopped red or green capsicum into the mixture with the milk and cheddar.*

STORAGE TIME: *Store the muffins in an airtight container for up to 2 days.*

Sift the flour and cornmeal into a large bowl and make a well in the centre.

Pour the milk mixture into the well in the dry ingredients and fold gently until just combined.

Spoon the dough into the muffin holes and bake until lightly golden.

Cheese soufflé

PREPARATION TIME: 10 MINUTES | TOTAL COOKING TIME: 35 MINUTES | SERVES 4

60 g (2¼ oz) butter
45 g (1½ oz) plain (all-purpose) flour
315 ml (11 fl oz/1¼ cups) milk, warmed
185 g (6½ oz/1½ cups) grated cheddar cheese
1 teaspoon dijon mustard
4 eggs, separated
1 tablespoon freshly grated parmesan cheese

1 Preheat the oven to 200°C (400°F/Gas 6). Brush a 1.5 litre (52 fl oz/6 cup) soufflé dish with melted butter or oil. Melt the butter in a large saucepan then add the flour. Stir over low heat for 2 minutes, or until the flour is lightly golden and bubbling. Remove from the heat and gradually add the milk, stirring until the mixture is smooth. Return the pan to the heat and stir constantly over low heat until the mixture boils and thickens. Simmer for 1 minute, then remove from the heat.

2 Add the grated cheddar, dijon mustard and egg yolks, and stir until the cheese has melted. Season to taste with salt and freshly ground black pepper. Cover the surface with plastic wrap to prevent a skin forming and leave the sauce to cool slightly.

3 Put the egg whites in a clean dry bowl and whisk until stiff peaks form. Using a metal spoon, fold one-third of the egg whites into the sauce, then gently fold in the remaining egg whites, being careful not to lose any volume. Gently pour the mixture into the prepared dish. Run your thumb or a knife around the inside edge of the dish to push the soufflé mixture slightly away from the edge—this will help the soufflé to rise evenly.

4 Sprinkle with the parmesan and bake the soufflé for 25–30 minutes, or until well risen and cooked through (cover it if it appears to be over-browning). Serve immediately.

Gently fold the egg whites into the sauce with a metal spoon.

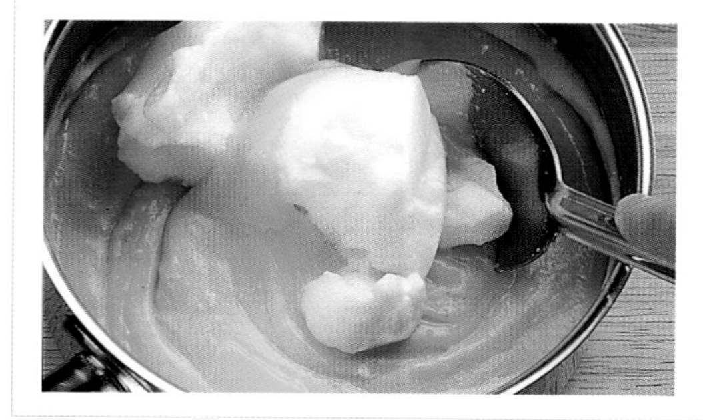

Run your thumb around the top of the soufflé to help it rise evenly.

NUTRITION PER SERVE
Protein 30 g; Fat 50 g; Carbohydrate 15 g; Dietary Fibre 0.5 g; Cholesterol 365 mg; 2655 kJ (635 Cal)

Scrambled eggs

PREPARATION TIME: 5 MINUTES | TOTAL COOKING TIME: 5 MINUTES | SERVES 2

6 eggs
1 tablespoon milk or pouring (whipping) cream
50 g (1¾ oz) butter
2 slices toast

1 Crack the eggs into a bowl, add the milk or cream and season well. Whisk gently with a fork until well combined.

2 Melt half the butter in a small saucepan or frying pan over low heat. Add the eggs, and stir constantly with a wooden spoon. Do not turn up the heat—scrambling must be slow and gentle. When most of the egg has set, add remaining butter and remove pan from heat. There should be enough heat left in the pan to finish cooking the eggs and melt the butter. Scrambled eggs should be creamy, not rubbery. Serve immediately—they will not sit even for a minute.

NOTE: *Use fresh eggs when scrambling. To check whether an egg is fresh put it in cold water. If it sinks on its side it is fresh, and if it floats on its end it is stale. If somewhere between it is not perfectly fresh but still good enough to use.*

VARIATIONS: *Scrambled eggs are also delicious with cheese such as gruyère or a handful of chopped fresh herbs.*

NUTRITION PER SERVE
Protein 20 g; Fat 35 g; Carbohydrate 15 g; Dietary Fibre 1 g; Cholesterol 605 mg; 1935 kJ (460 Cal)

Break up the eggs with a fork and stir gently until well combined.

Pour in the eggs and stir constantly with a wooden spoon.

When the eggs are nearly set, add the butter and remove from the heat.

Ricotta pancakes with goat's milk yoghurt and pears

PREPARATION TIME: 15 MINUTES | TOTAL COOKING TIME: 50 MINUTES | SERVES 4

185 g (6½ oz/1½ cups) plain (all-purpose) flour
2 teaspoons baking powder
2 teaspoons ground ginger
2 tablespoons caster (superfine) sugar
4 eggs, separated
350 g (12 oz) low-fat ricotta cheese
1 pear, peeled, cored and grated
310 ml (10¾ fl oz/1¼ cups) milk
40 g (1½ oz) butter
3 beurre bosc pears, unpeeled
40 g (1½ oz) butter
1 tablespoon soft brown sugar
1 teaspoon ground cinnamon
200 g (7 oz) goat's milk yoghurt

NUTRITION PER SERVE
Protein 26 g; Fat 41 g; Carbohydrate 85 g; Dietary Fibre 5.5 g; Cholesterol 266 mg; 3341 kJ (799 Cal)

1 Sift the flour, baking powder, ginger and sugar into a bowl and make a well in the centre. Pour the combined egg yolks, ricotta, pear and milk into the well and mix together until smooth.

2 Beat the egg whites until soft peaks form, then fold into the mixture.

3 Heat a frying pan over medium heat and melt some of the butter. Pour 3 tablespoons of the batter into the pan and swirl gently to create an even pancake. Cook for 1–1½ minutes, or until bubbles form on the surface, then turn and cook the other side for 1 minute, or until golden. Repeat with the remaining butter and mixture to make 11 more pancakes. Keep warm.

4 Cut the pears into thick slices lengthways. Melt the butter in a frying pan and add the sugar and cinnamon, then stir until the sugar dissolves. Add the pears and cook in batches, turning once, until golden and tender. Serve stacks of pancakes with the pears and yoghurt.

Stir the combined egg yolks, ricotta, grated pear and milk into the flour.

Cook the pancake until bubbles form on the surface, then turn over.

Cook the pears in batches in the buttery sauce, turning to coat in the mixture.

Mini frittatas

PREPARATION TIME: 30 MINUTES | TOTAL COOKING TIME: 45 MINUTES | MAKES 12

1 kg (2 lb 4 oz) orange sweet potato
1 tablespoon oil
30 g (1 oz) butter
4 leeks, white part only, finely sliced
2 garlic cloves, crushed
250 g (9 oz) feta cheese, crumbled
8 eggs
125 ml (4 fl oz/½ cup) pouring (whipping) cream

1 Preheat the oven to 180°C (350°F/Gas 4). Grease or brush twelve 250 ml (9 fl oz/1 cup) muffin holes with oil or melted butter. Cut small rounds of baking paper and place into the base of each hole. Cut the sweet potato into small cubes and boil, steam or microwave until tender. Drain well and set aside.

2 Heat the oil and butter in a frying pan and cook the leek for 10 minutes, stirring occasionally, or until very soft and lightly golden. Add the garlic and cook for a further 1 minute. Cool, then stir in the feta and sweet potato. Divide among the muffin holes.

3 Whisk the eggs and cream together and season with salt and freshly ground black pepper. Pour the egg mixture into each hole until three-quarters filled, then press the vegetables down gently. Bake for 25–30 minutes, or until golden and set. Leave in the tins for 5 minutes, then ease out with a knife. Delicious either served hot or at room temperature.

Cut small rounds of baking paper and put one in the base of each muffin hole.

Whisk the eggs and cream together, season and pour into the muffin holes.

NUTRITION PER FRITTATA
Protein 10 g; Fat 15 g; Carbohydrate 13 g; Dietary Fibre 2.5 g; Cholesterol 155 mg; 1000 kJ (240 Cal)

Hash browns

PREPARATION TIME: 30 MINUTES | TOTAL COOKING TIME: 15–20 MINUTES | SERVES 4

800 g (1 lb 12 oz) waxy potatoes (such as Desiree or Pontiac), peeled
120 g (4¼ oz) butter

1 Boil or steam the potatoes until just tender. Drain, cool, chop coarsely and season with salt and freshly ground black pepper.

2 Heat half the butter in a large heavy-based frying pan and put four lightly greased egg rings into the pan. Spoon the potato evenly into the egg rings, filling the rings to the top and pressing the potato down lightly to form flat cakes. Cook over medium-low heat for 5–7 minutes, or until a crust forms on the bottom. Be careful not to burn. Shake the pan gently to prevent sticking.

3 Turn the hash browns with a large spatula. Gently loosen the egg rings and remove with tongs. Cook for another 4–5 minutes, or until browned and crisp. Remove from the pan and drain on paper towels. Add a little more butter to the pan, if necessary, and cook the remaining potato in the same way. Serve immediately.

NOTE: *If you don't have egg rings, cook as one large cake.*

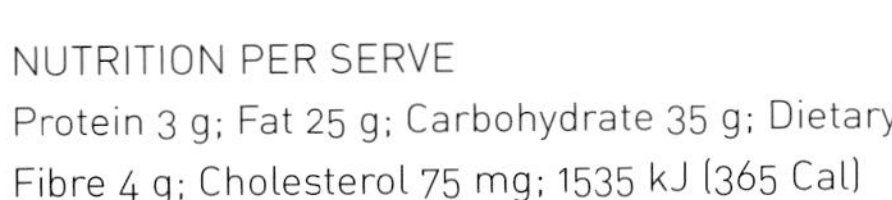
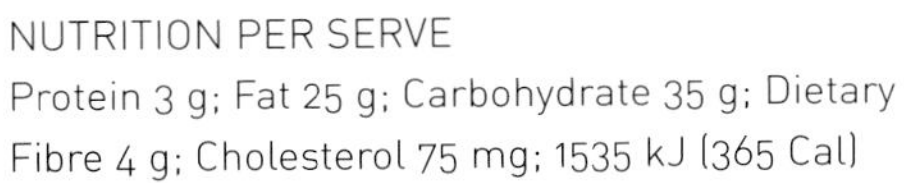

NUTRITION PER SERVE
Protein 3 g; Fat 25 g; Carbohydrate 35 g; Dietary Fibre 4 g; Cholesterol 75 mg; 1535 kJ (365 Cal)

Fill the egg rings with the chopped potato and press the mixture down lightly.

Cook until a crust forms on the bottom. Be careful to prevent burning or sticking.

Use a large spatula to turn the hash brown over once a crust has formed on the bottom.

Snacks

Tempura vegetables with wasabi mayonnaise

PREPARATION TIME: 20 MINUTES | TOTAL COOKING TIME: 20 MINUTES | SERVES 4–6

WASABI MAYONNAISE
2 tablespoons mayonnaise
3 teaspoons wasabi paste
½ teaspoon grated lime zest

1 egg, separated
125 g (4½ oz/1 cup) plain (all-purpose) flour
oil, for deep-frying
1 small (250 g/9 oz) eggplant (aubergine), sliced 5 mm (¼ inch) thick
1 large onion, sliced 5 mm (¼ inch) thick, with rings intact
300 g (10½ oz) orange sweet potato, peeled and sliced 5 mm (¼ inch) thick

1 To make the wasabi mayonnaise, mix together all the ingredients. Cover with plastic wrap and refrigerate until ready to use.

2 For tempura batter, whisk the egg yolk, add 1 cup iced water and stir to combine. Add the flour and, using chopsticks, gently stir until just starting to combine (the batter should still contain lumps). In a separate bowl whisk the egg white until soft peaks form, then gently fold through the batter.

3 Heat the oil in a large, deep saucepan or deep-fryer to 180°C (350°F). Dust vegetables in flour and dip in tempura batter. Deep-fry for 2–3 minutes, or until crisp. Drain on crumpled paper towels and serve immediately with the wasabi mayonnaise.

NUTRITION PER SERVE (6)
Protein 5.2 g; Fat 6.5g; Carbohydrate 26.1 g; Dietary Fibre 3.0 g; Cholesterol 33 mg; 812 kJ (194 Cal)

Gently stir the combined water and egg yolk into the flour mixture.

Pick up two different pieces of vegetable with tongs and dip into the batter.

Deep-fry the battered vegetables until they are golden brown and cooked through.

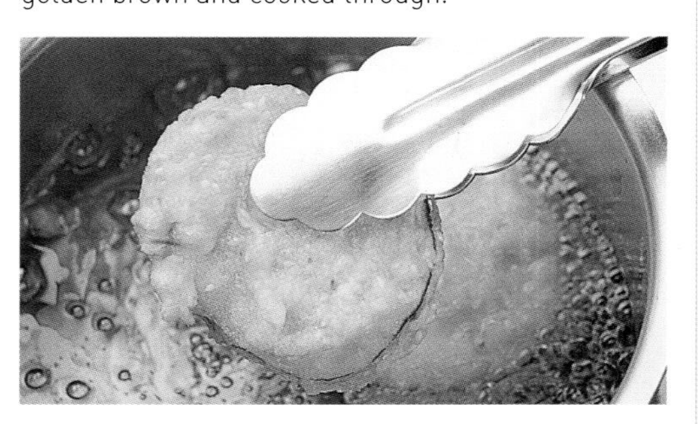

Marinated chilli mushrooms

PREPARATION TIME: 20 MINUTES + OVERNIGHT REFRIGERATION | TOTAL COOKING TIME: NIL | SERVES 8 (AS PART OF AN ANTIPASTO PLATTER, SEE HINT)

750 g (1 lb 10 oz) button mushrooms
500 ml (17 fl oz/2 cups) olive oil
2 tablespoons lemon juice
1 garlic clove, finely chopped
¼ teaspoon caster (superfine) sugar
1 red chilli, finely chopped
1 green chilli, finely chopped
1 tablespoon chopped coriander (cilantro)
1 tablespoon chopped flat-leaf (Italian) parsley

1 Wipe the mushrooms clean with a damp paper towel and put in a bowl.

2 Mix together the oil, lemon juice, garlic, sugar and chilli. Pour over the mushrooms and mix well. Cover with plastic wrap and marinate in the refrigerator overnight.

3 Just before serving, add the herbs, season and mix well.

NOTE: *The coriander and parsley are added just before serving so that they keep their colour. However, if you prefer a stronger flavour, add them before marinating.*

HINT: *Serve as part of an antipasto platter, with a selection of sun-dried vegetables, marinated artichokes, caperberries and toasted bruschetta.*

Wipe the mushrooms with a damp paper towel to remove any dirt.

Pour the combined oil, lemon juice, garlic, sugar and chilli over the mushrooms.

NUTRITION PER SERVE
Protein 3.5 g; Fat 1.5 g; Carbohydrate 2 g; Dietary Fibre 2.5 g; Cholesterol 0 mg; 150 kJ (35 Cal)

Labneh (yoghurt cheese)

PREPARATION TIME: 20 MINUTES + 4 DAYS REFRIGERATION | TOTAL COOKING TIME: NIL | MAKES 24

1 kg (2 lb 4 oz) Greek yoghurt
375 ml (13 fl oz/1½ cups) extra virgin olive oil
2 garlic cloves, chopped
2 tablespoons rosemary leaves
6–8 sprigs thyme

1 Put the yoghurt in a bowl and season with 2 teaspoons salt and 1 teaspoon freshly ground black pepper. Line a bowl with a piece of muslin folded in half to make a 45 cm (18 inch) square. Spoon the yoghurt mixture into the centre. Bring the corners together and, using a long piece of kitchen string, tie as closely as possible to the yoghurt, leaving a loop at the end.

2 Thread the loop through the handle of a wooden spoon and hang the yoghurt over a bowl to drain in the fridge for 3 days.

3 Mix the oil, garlic, rosemary and thyme together. Untie the muslin and roll tablespoons of drained yoghurt into balls (they won't be completely smooth). Make sure your hands are cool, and wash them often. Rinse a large wide-necked jar with boiling water and dry in a warm oven. Put the labneh in the jar and cover with the herbed olive oil. Cover and refrigerate for 24 hours. Return to room temperature and serve with bread. Store in the fridge for up to 1 week.

Spoon the seasoned yoghurt into the centre of the muslin square.

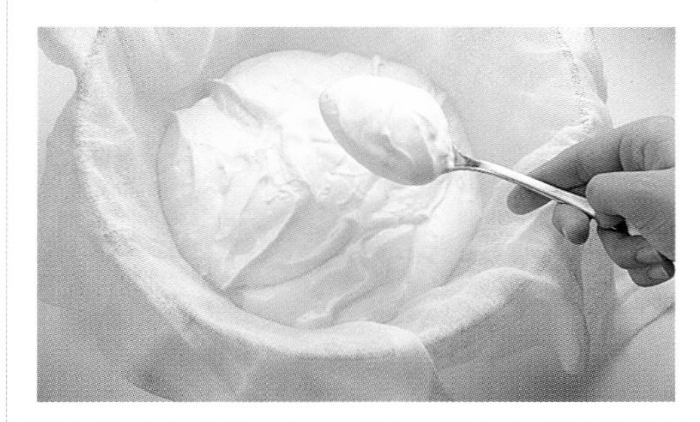

Thread the loop through the handle of a wooden spoon to hang the yoghurt.

NUTRITION PER PIECE
Protein 2 g; Fat 6.5 g; Carbohydrate 2 g; Dietary Fibre 0 g; Cholesterol 6.5 mg; 312 kJ (75 Cal)

Camembert and potato terrine

PREPARATION TIME: 1 HOUR + OVERNIGHT REFRIGERATION | TOTAL COOKING TIME: 50 MINUTES | SERVES 8

1 kg (2 lb 4 oz) new potatoes, unpeeled
3 granny smith apples
125 g (4½ oz) butter
3 tablespoons olive oil
200 g (7 oz) camembert, chilled and very thinly sliced
2 tablespoons chopped parsley

NUTRITION PER SERVE
Protein 8 g; Fat 25 g; Carbohydrate 20 g; Dietary Fibre 3 g; Cholesterol 65 mg; 1456 kJ (350 Cal)

1 Boil the potatoes in a large saucepan of salted water for about 15 minutes, or until soft. Drain and cool, then peel and cut into slices 1 cm (½ inch) thick. Core and slice the apples into 5 mm (¼ inch) thick rounds. Heat half the butter and half the oil in a frying pan and cook the potato until just golden. Drain on paper towels. Heat the remaining butter and oil. Lightly fry the apple until golden. Drain on paper towels.

2 Line a 25 x 11 cm (10 x 4¼ inch) terrine with baking paper. Preheat the oven to 180°C (350°F/Gas 4).

3 Arrange a layer of potato in the base of the terrine. Add a layer of apple and then camembert. Sprinkle with the parsley and season well. Build up the layers, finishing with potato.

4 Lightly oil a piece of foil and cover the terrine, sealing well. Put the terrine in a baking dish and half-fill the dish with water. Bake for 20 minutes. Remove from the oven and cover the terrine with a piece of cardboard. Put weights or food tins on top of the cardboard to compress the terrine. Refrigerate overnight. Turn out and cut into slices to serve.

Slice the apples into thick rounds and fry in the butter and oil until golden.

Arrange the potato, apple and camembert in layers in the terrine.

Cover the terrine with cardboard and put heavy tins on top to compress it overnight.

Vegetable chips

PREPARATION TIME: 20 MINUTES | TOTAL COOKING TIME: 15 MINUTES | SERVES 6–8

250 g (9 oz) orange sweet potato
250 g (9 oz) beetroot (beets), peeled
250 g (9 oz) potato
oil, for deep-frying

1 Preheat the oven to 180°C (350°F/Gas 4). Run a sharp vegetable peeler along the length of the sweet potato to create ribbons. Cut the beetroot into paper-thin slices with a sharp vegetable peeler or knife. Cut the potato into thin slices, using a mandolin slicer or knife with a crinkle-cut blade (see NOTE).

2 Fill a deep heavy-based saucepan one-third full with oil and heat until a cube of bread dropped into the oil browns in 10 seconds. Cook the vegetables in batches for about 30 seconds, or until golden and crispy. You may need to turn them with tongs or a long-handled metal spoon. Drain on paper towels and season with salt.

3 Place all the vegetable chips on a baking tray and keep warm in the oven while cooking the remaining vegetables.

NOTE: *If you don't have a mandolin or crinkle-cut knife at home, simply use a sharp knife to cut fine slices. The cooking time for the chips will remain the same.*

NUTRITION PER SERVE (8)
Protein 2 g; Fat 5 g; Carbohydrate 12 g; Dietary Fibre 2 g; Cholesterol 0 mg; 413 kJ (99 Cal)

Use a sharp vegetable peeler to peel thin strips of sweet potato.

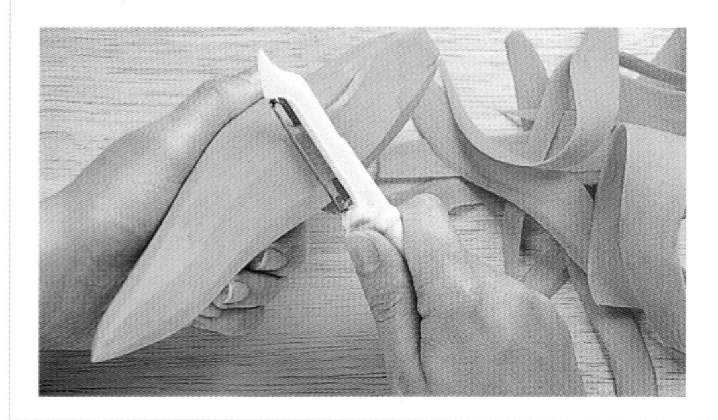

If you have a mandolin, use it for slicing the potatoes very finely.

Deep-fry the vegetables in batches until they are golden and crispy.

Blue cheese and port pâté

PREPARATION TIME: 10 MINUTES + REFRIGERATION | TOTAL COOKING TIME: NIL | SERVES 8

350 g (12 oz) cream cheese, at room temperature
60 g (2 oz) unsalted butter, softened
4 tablespoons port
300 g (10½ oz) blue cheese, at room temperature, mashed
1 tablespoon snipped chives
45 g (1½ oz) walnut halves

1 Using electric beaters, beat the cream cheese and butter until smooth, then stir in the port. Add the blue cheese and chives and stir until just combined. Season to taste.

2 Spoon the mixture into a serving bowl and smooth the surface. Cover the pâté with plastic wrap and refrigerate until firm.

3 Arrange the walnuts over the top of the pâté, pressing down lightly. Serve at room temperature with crusty bread and celery stalks.

Stir the blue cheese and chives into the cream cheese and butter mixture.

Arrange the walnut halves over the surface, pressing down lightly.

NUTRITION PER SERVE
Protein 12 g; Fat 37 g; Carbohydrate 2.5 g; Dietary Fibre 0.5 g; Cholesterol 100 mg; 1650 kJ (395 cal)

Falafel with tomato salsa

PREPARATION TIME: 40 MINUTES + 4 HOURS SOAKING + 30 MINUTES STANDING | TOTAL COOKING TIME: 20 MINUTES | SERVES 8

440 g (15½ oz/2 cups) dried chickpeas
1 small onion, finely chopped
2 garlic cloves, crushed
4 tablespoons chopped flat-leaf (Italian) parsley
2 tablespoons chopped coriander (cilantro) leaves
2 teaspoons ground cumin
½ teaspoon baking powder
oil, for deep-frying

TOMATO SALSA
2 tomatoes
¼ Lebanese (short) cucumber, finely chopped
½ green capsicum (pepper), diced
2 tablespoons chopped flat-leaf (Italian) parsley
1 teaspoon sugar
2 teaspoons chilli sauce
½ teaspoon grated lemon zest
2 tablespoons lemon juice

1 Soak the chickpeas in 1 litre (35 fl oz/4 cups) water for 4 hours or overnight. Drain. Place in a food processor and blend for 30 seconds, or until finely ground. Add the onion, garlic, parsley, coriander, cumin, baking powder and 1 tablespoon water, then process for 10 seconds to make a rough paste. Leave, covered, for 30 minutes.

2 To make the salsa, score a cross in the base of each tomato. Put them in a bowl of boiling water for 30 seconds, then plunge into cold water and peel the skin away from the cross. Finely chop, then place in a bowl with all the other ingredients and mix well.

3 Using your hands, shape heaped tablespoons of the falafel mixture into even-sized balls. If there is any excess liquid, squeeze it out. Fill a large heavy-based saucepan one-third full with oil and heat until a cube of bread dropped into the oil browns in 15 seconds.

4 Lower the falafel balls into the oil and cook in batches of five for 3–4 minutes, or until well browned all over. Remove the falafel with a slotted spoon and drain on paper towels. Serve hot or cold on a bed of the tomato salsa, with pitta bread.

NUTRITION PER SERVE
Protein 10.5 g; Fat 8 g; Carbohydrate 22.5 g; Dietary Fibre 8 g; Cholesterol 0 mg; 855 kJ (204 Cal)

Grind the drained chickpeas in a food processor until finely chopped.

Shape heaped tablespoons of the falafel mixture into even-sized balls.

Cook until well browned, then remove them with a slotted spoon and drain.

Vietnamese rice rolls

PREPARATION TIME: 30 MINUTES + 10 MINUTES STANDING | TOTAL COOKING TIME: 10 MINUTES | SERVES 4

75 g (2½ oz) dried rice vermicelli
200 g (7 oz) firm tofu
1 teaspoon sesame oil
1 tablespoon peanut oil
1 packet 15 cm (6 inch) square rice-paper wrappers
½ small Lebanese (short) cucumber, cut into matchstick strips
½ carrot, cut into matchsticks
1 large handful mint
50 g (1¾ oz/⅓ cup) roasted salted cashews, roughly chopped
3 tablespoons hoisin sauce
2 tablespoons kecap manis (see NOTE)
1 tablespoon lime juice

1 Place the vermicelli in a bowl, cover with boiling water and leave for 10 minutes. Drain well.

2 Pat the tofu dry and cut into four slices. Heat the oils in a large frying pan and cook the tofu over medium heat for 3 minutes on each side, or until golden. Drain on paper towels. Cut each slice into four widthways.

3 Fill a bowl with warm water. Dip one wrapper at a time into the water for about 15 seconds, or until pliable. Place the wrapper on a work surface, top with some vermicelli, tofu, cucumber, carrot, mint and cashews. Roll tightly, folding in the sides and put on a plate, seam side down. Cover with a damp cloth and repeat.

4 To make the dipping sauce, place the hoisin sauce, kecap manis and lime juice in a bowl and mix. Serve immediately with the spring rolls.

NOTE: *Kecap manis is a thick, sweet soy sauce. If you can't find it, use regular soy sauce mixed with a little soft brown sugar.*

Cook the tofu over medium heat, turning once, until golden brown on both sides.

Fold the sides of the wrappers in and roll up tightly, enclosing the filling.

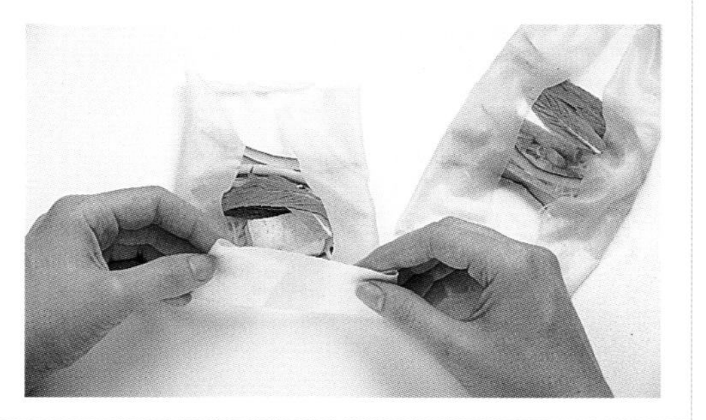

NUTRITION PER SERVE
Protein 6 g; Fat 12 g; Carbohydrate 16 g; Dietary Fibre 2 g; Cholesterol 0 mg; 580 kJ (136 Cal)

Dolmades

PREPARATION TIME: 1 HOUR + 1 HOUR SOAKING | TOTAL COOKING TIME: 1 HOUR | MAKES 42

275 g (9¾ oz) vine leaves in brine
185 ml (6 fl oz/¾ cup) olive oil
2 onions, finely chopped
165 g (5¾ oz/¾ cup) short-grain rice
6 spring onions (scallions), finely chopped
1 large handful chopped dill
1 tablespoon chopped mint
1 tablespoon lemon juice

1 Rinse the vine leaves in cold water, soak in warm water for 1 hour and then drain.

2 Heat 125 ml (4 fl oz/½ cup) oil in a heavy-based saucepan. Add the onion and cook over low heat for 5 minutes. Remove from the heat, cover and leave for 5 minutes. Mix in the rice, spring onion, herbs and lemon juice.

3 Lay out a vine leaf, vein side up, on a plate. Place 3 teaspoons of filling on the centre. Fold the sides over the mixture, then roll up towards the tip of the leaf. Repeat to make 42 dolmades.

4 Use five or six vine leaves to line the base of a large heavy-based saucepan. Pack the dolmades in the lined pan in two layers and drizzle with the remaining oil. Put a plate on top of the dolmades, to keep them in place, and cover with 375 ml (13 fl oz/1½ cups) water. Bring to the boil, reduce the heat and simmer, covered, for 45 minutes. Remove the plate, lift out the dolmades with a slotted spoon and drizzle with lemon juice. Serve either warm or cold with lemon wedges, if desired.

NOTE: *Fresh vine leaves can be used, if available. Use small leaves, blanched briefly in boiling water.*

NUTRITION PER DOLMADE
Protein 2 g; Fat 4.5 g; Carbohydrate 3 g; Dietary Fibre 0 g; Cholesterol 0 mg; 220 kJ (50 Cal)

Fold the sides of the vine leaf over the filling and roll up towards the tip of the leaf.

Cover the dolmades with a plate to keep them in place, then pour in the water.

Bean nachos

PREPARATION TIME: 20 MINUTES | TOTAL COOKING TIME: 10 MINUTES | SERVES 4

4 large ripe tomatoes
2 ripe avocados, mashed
1 tablespoon lime juice
1 tablespoon sweet chilli sauce
1 tablespoon oil
2 small red onions, diced
1 small red chilli, chopped
2 teaspoons ground oregano
2 teaspoons ground cumin
¼ teaspoon chilli powder
1 tablespoon tomato paste (concentrated purée)
250 ml (9 fl oz/1 cup) dry white wine
2 x 440 g (15½ oz) tins red kidney beans, drained and rinsed
3 tablespoons chopped coriander (cilantro) leaves
200 g (7 oz) corn chips
90 g (3¼ oz/⅔ cup) grated cheddar cheese
sour cream, to serve

1 Score a cross in the base of each tomato. Put them in a bowl of boiling water for 30 seconds, then plunge into cold water and peel the skin away from the cross. Cut in half and scoop out the seeds with a teaspoon. Chop the tomato flesh.

2 Mix together the avocado, lime juice and sweet chilli sauce.

3 Heat the oil in a large frying pan. Cook the onion, chilli, oregano, cumin and chilli powder over medium heat for 2 minutes. Add the tomato, tomato paste and wine and cook for 5 minutes, or until the liquid reduces. Add the beans and coriander.

4 Divide the corn chips into four portions on heatproof plates. Top with the bean mixture and sprinkle with cheese. Flash under a hot grill (broiler) until the cheese melts. Serve with the avocado mixture and sour cream.

NUTRITION PER SERVE
Protein 26 g; Fat 35 g; Carbohydrate 53 g; Dietary Fibre 20 g; Cholesterol 20 mg; 2845 kJ (680 Cal)

Scoop out the seeds of the tomatoes and roughly chop the flesh.

Cook the onion, chilli, oregano and spices in a large frying pan.

Cook the mixture until the liquid is reduced and the tomato is soft.

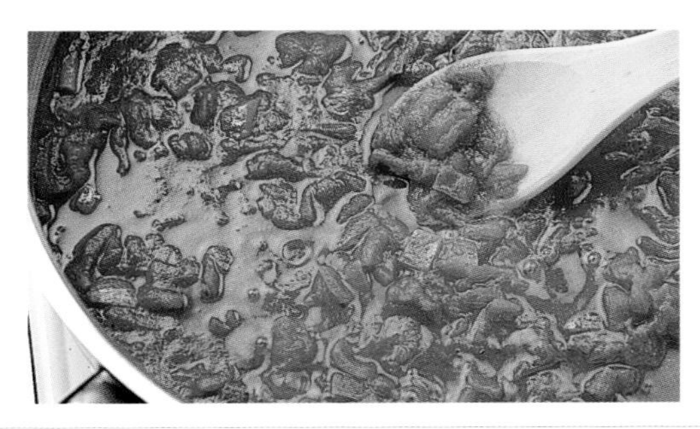

Baked herbed feta

PREPARATION TIME: 10 MINUTES | TOTAL COOKING TIME: 15 MINUTES | SERVES 6

300 g (10½ oz) piece of feta cheese
1 tablespoon chopped rosemary
1 tablespoon chopped oregano
1 tablespoon chopped thyme
2 tablespoons olive oil

1 Preheat the oven to 180°C (350°F/Gas 4). Put the feta on a piece of foil about 30 cm (12 inches) square. Mix together the rosemary, oregano and thyme, and press onto the sides of the feta. Drizzle with the oil and season to taste with freshly ground black pepper. Gently fold the sides and ends of the foil over to make a parcel.

2 Place on a baking tray and bake for 10–15 minutes, or until the feta is soft. Drain off any excess liquid before serving. Serve hot or cold, with bread or as part of a cheese platter or salad.

NOTE: *If the piece of feta is thick, it may need an extra 5 minutes in the oven to heat through.*

STORAGE: *Cover any leftovers with plastic wrap and store in the fridge for up to 2 days.*

NUTRITION PER SERVE
Protein 9 g; Fat 20 g; Carbohydrate 0 g; Dietary Fibre 0 g; Cholesterol 35 mg; 820 kJ (195 Cal)

Using a sharp knife, finely chop the rosemary, oregano and thyme.

Press the combined herbs onto the sides of the piece of feta.

Fold the foil firmly over the feta to make a secure parcel and then bake until the cheese is soft.

Semi-dried tomatoes

PREPARATION TIME: 10 MINUTES + 24 HOURS REFRIGERATION | TOTAL COOKING TIME: 2 HOURS 30 MINUTES | FILLS A 500 ML (16 FL OZ) JAR

16 roma (plum) tomatoes
3 tablespoons thyme, chopped
2 tablespoons olive oil

1 Preheat the oven to 160°C (315°F/Gas 2–3). Cut the tomatoes into quarters lengthways and lay them skin side down on a wire rack in a baking tray.

2 Sprinkle with 1 teaspoon of salt, 1 teaspoon of freshly ground black pepper and the thyme and cook in the oven for 2½ hours. Check occasionally to make sure the tomatoes don't burn.

3 Toss the tomatoes in the olive oil and leave to cool before packing into sterilised jars and sealing. Store in the refrigerator for 24 hours before using. Semi-dried (sun-blushed) tomatoes should be eaten within 3–4 days.

NOTE: *To sterilise a storage jar, rinse with boiling water then place in a warm oven until completely dry. Do not dry with a tea towel (dish towel).*

NUTRITION PER SERVE
It is not possible to make a nutritional analysis for this recipe.

Cut the tomatoes into quarters and lay them skin side down on a wire rack.

Season the tomatoes with salt, freshly ground black pepper and fresh thyme.

Cover the tomatoes with olive oil and toss until well coated.

Vegetable frittata with hummus and black olives

PREPARATION TIME: 35 MINUTES | TOTAL COOKING TIME: 40 MINUTES | MAKES 30 PIECES

- 2 large red capsicums (peppers)
- 600 g (1 lb 5 oz) orange sweet potato, cut into 1 cm (½ inch) slices
- 3 tablespoons olive oil
- 2 leeks, white part only, finely sliced
- 2 garlic cloves, crushed
- 250 g (9 oz) zucchini (courgettes), thinly sliced
- 500 g (1 lb 2 oz) eggplant (aubergine), cut into 1 cm (½ inch) slices
- 8 eggs, lightly beaten
- 2 tablespoons finely chopped basil
- 125 g (4½ oz/1¼ cups) grated parmesan cheese
- 200 g (7 oz) hummus
- black olives, pitted and halved, to garnish

NUTRITION PER PIECE
Protein 4.5 g; Fat 6 g; Carbohydrates 5 g; Dietary Fibre 2 g; Cholesterol 52 mg; 387 kJ (92 Cal)

1 Cut the capsicums into large pieces, removing the seeds and membrane. Place, skin side up, under a hot grill (broiler) until the skin blackens and blisters. Cool in a plastic bag, then peel.

2 Cook the sweet potato in a saucepan of boiling water for 4–5 minutes, or until just tender. Drain.

3 Heat 1 tablespoon of the oil in a deep round 23 cm (9 inch) frying pan and stir the leek and garlic over medium heat for 1 minute, or until soft. Add the zucchini and cook for 2 minutes, then remove from the pan.

4 Heat the remaining oil in the same pan and cook the eggplant in batches for 2 minutes on each side, or until golden. Line the base of the pan with half the eggplant and spread with the leek mixture. Cover with the roasted capsicum, then with the remaining eggplant and finally the sweet potato.

5 Put the eggs, basil and parmesan in a bowl. Season with freshly ground black pepper, mix well and pour over the vegetables. Cook over low heat for 15 minutes, or until almost cooked. Place the pan under a hot grill for 2–3 minutes, or until golden and cooked. Cool before inverting onto a board. Trim the edges and cut into 30 squares. Top each square with a dollop of hummus and half an olive.

Lay the roasted capsicum pieces over the leek and zucchini mixture.

Pour the egg mixture over the vegetables so that they are covered.

Cook the frittata under a hot grill until it is golden brown on top.

Garlic and herb marinated artichokes

PREPARATION TIME: 20 MINUTES + OVERNIGHT REFRIGERATION | TOTAL COOKING TIME: NIL | SERVES 8 (AS PART OF AN ANTIPASTO PLATTER)

2 garlic cloves, chopped
125 ml (4 fl oz/½ cup) olive oil
2 tablespoons finely chopped dill
3 tablespoons finely chopped parsley
2 tablespoons finely chopped basil
2 tablespoons lemon juice
2 x 400 g (14 oz) tinned artichokes
40 g (1½ oz/¼ cup) finely diced red capsicum (pepper)

1 To make the marinade, whisk together the garlic, oil, herbs and lemon juice in a bowl. Season with salt and freshly ground black pepper.

2 Drain the artichokes and add to the bowl with the capsicum. Mix well to coat. Cover and marinate in the refrigerator overnight. Serve as part of an antipasto platter or use in salads.

STORAGE TIME: *The artichokes will keep in an airtight container in the refrigerator for up to 1 week.*

NUTRITION PER SERVE
Protein 1 g; Fat 7.5 g; Carbohydrate 1 g; Dietary Fibre 1.5 g; Cholesterol 0 mg; 320 kJ (75 Cal)

Finely chop the fresh herbs. You will need dill, parsley and basil.

Combine the garlic, oil, herbs and lemon juice to make the marinade.

Drain the artichokes well before adding to the marinade. Marinate in the fridge overnight.

California rolls

PREPARATION TIME: 35 MINUTES + 15 MINUTES STANDING | TOTAL COOKING TIME: 15 MINUTES | MAKES 30

500 g (1 lb 2 oz) short-grain white rice
3 tablespoons rice vinegar
1 tablespoon caster (superfine) sugar
5 sheets nori (dried seaweed)
1 large Lebanese (short) cucumber, cut lengthways into long batons
1 avocado, thinly sliced
1 tablespoon black sesame seeds, toasted
30 g (1 oz) pickled ginger slices
125 g (4½ oz/½ cup) mayonnaise
3 teaspoons wasabi paste
2 teaspoons soy sauce

1 Wash the rice under cold running water, tossing, until the water runs clear. Put the rice and 750 ml (26 fl oz/3 cups) water in a saucepan. Bring to the boil over low heat and cook for 5 minutes, or until tunnels form in the rice. Remove from the heat, cover and leave for 15 minutes.

2 Place the vinegar, sugar and 1 teaspoon salt in a small saucepan and stir over low heat until the sugar and salt dissolve.

3 Transfer the rice to a non-metallic bowl and use a wooden spoon to separate the grains. Make a slight well in the centre, slowly stir in the vinegar dressing, then cool a little.

4 Lay a nori sheet, shiny side down, on a bamboo mat or flat surface and spread out one-fifth of the rice, leaving a narrow clear border at one end. Arrange one-fifth of the cucumber, avocado, sesame seeds and ginger lengthways over the rice, keeping away from the border. Spread on some of the combined mayonnaise, wasabi and soy sauce and roll to cover the filling. Continue rolling tightly to join the edge, then hold in place for a few seconds. Trim the ends and cut into slices. Serve with wasabi mayonnaise.

NUTRITION PER PIECE
Protein 1.5 g; Fat 3 g; Carbohydrate 15 g; Dietary Fibre 1 g; Cholesterol 1.5 mg; 380 kJ (90 Cal)

Cook the rice until tunnels appear, then cover and leave for 15 minutes.

Spread the wasabi mayonnaise mixture over the vegetables and start rolling.

Onion bhajis with spicy tomato sauce

PREPARATION TIME: 30 MINUTES | TOTAL COOKING TIME: 35 MINUTES | MAKES ABOUT 25

SPICY TOMATO SAUCE
2–3 red chillies, chopped
1 red capsicum (pepper), diced
425 g (15 oz) tin chopped tomatoes
2 garlic cloves, finely chopped
2 tablespoons soft brown sugar
1½ tablespoons cider vinegar

125 g (4½ oz/1 cup) plain (all-purpose) flour
2 teaspoons baking powder
½ teaspoon chilli powder
½ teaspoon ground turmeric
1 teaspoon ground cumin
2 eggs, beaten
2 very large handfuls chopped coriander (cilantro) leaves
4 onions, very thinly sliced
oil, for deep-frying

1 To make the sauce, combine all the ingredients with 3 tablespoons water in a saucepan. Bring to the boil, then reduce the heat and simmer for 20 minutes, or until the mixture thickens. Remove from the heat.

2 To make the bhajis, sift the flour, baking powder, spices and 1 teaspoon of salt into a bowl and make a well in the centre. Gradually add the combined egg and 3 tablespoons water, whisking to make a smooth batter. Stir in the coriander and onion.

3 Fill a deep, heavy-based saucepan one-third full with oil and heat until a cube of bread dropped into the oil browns in 15 seconds. Drop dessertspoons of the mixture into the oil and cook in batches for 90 seconds on each side, or until golden. Drain on paper towels. Serve with the spicy tomato sauce.

NUTRITION PER BHAJI
Protein 1.5 g; Fat 2 g; Carbohydrate 7 g; Dietary Fibre 1 g; Cholesterol 14 mg; 218 kJ (52 Cal)

Peel the four onions and use a sharp knife to slice them very thinly.

Whisk together a smooth batter, then add the coriander and sliced onion and stir to coat.

Drop spoonfuls of the onion batter into the oil and cook in batches until golden.

Potato noodle nibbles

PREPARATION TIME: 30 MINUTES + COOLING | TOTAL COOKING TIME: 40 MINUTES | SERVES 4–6

450 g (1 lb) roasting (floury) potatoes, chopped
40 g (1½ oz) butter, softened
2 tablespoons grated parmesan or pecorino cheese
100 g (3½ oz) besan (chickpea) flour
2 teaspoons ground cumin
2 teaspoons garam masala
1 teaspoon ground coriander
1 teaspoon chilli powder
1 teaspoon cayenne pepper
1½ teaspoons ground turmeric
vegetable oil, for frying

1 Boil the potato until tender. Drain and cool for 15–20 minutes, then mash with the butter and cheese. Add the besan, cumin, garam masala, coriander, chilli powder, cayenne pepper, turmeric and ¾ teaspoon of salt. Mix with a wooden spoon until a soft, light dough forms. Turn out and knead lightly 10–12 times, until smooth.

2 Fill a large saucepan with vegetable oil to a depth of at least 10 cm (4 inches) and heat to 190°C (375°F). Test the temperature by dropping a small ball of dough into the oil. It is ready if the dough rises straight to the surface.

3 Using a piping bag with a 1 cm (½ inch) star nozzle, pipe short lengths of dough into the oil, in manageable batches. They will rise to the surface and turn golden quickly. Remove them with a slotted spoon and drain on paper towels. Serve within 2 hours, as a snack or to accompany drinks.

Boil the potato until tender and then mash with the butter and cheese.

Pipe short lengths of the dough into the hot oil. They will rise to the surface quickly.

NUTRITION PER SERVE (6)
Protein 7 g; Fat 15 g; Carbohydrate 20 g; Dietary Fibre 4 g; Cholesterol 20 mg; 1050 kJ (250 Cal)

Marinated bocconcini

PREPARATION TIME: 15 MINUTES + 3 DAYS REFRIGERATION | TOTAL COOKING TIME: 5 MINUTES | SERVES 8

400 g (14 oz) bocconcini (fresh baby mozzarella cheese), sliced
150 g (5½ oz) sun-dried capsicums (peppers) in oil
2 large handfuls small basil leaves
310 ml (10¾ fl oz/1¼ cups) virgin olive oil
60 ml (2 fl oz/¼ cup) lemon juice

1 Dry the bocconcini with paper towels. Drain the capsicums, retaining the oil in a pan, and cut into strips. Gently crush the basil leaves. Pour 250 ml (9 fl oz/1 cup) of the olive oil into the pan with the capsicum oil and gently heat for 5 minutes. Stir the lemon juice into the warmed oil.

2 Put a layer of bocconcini slices in a wide-necked 750 ml (24 fl oz/3 cup) sterilised clip-top jar. Sprinkle with freshly ground black pepper. Put a thin layer of basil leaves on top of the cheese and cover with some of the capsicum. Continue layering, then cover with the warmed oil, using the remaining olive oil if necessary. Seal the jar and marinate in the refrigerator for 3 days. Return to room temperature and drain before serving.

NOTE: *To sterilise a storage jar, rinse with boiling water then place in a warm oven until completely dry. Don't dry with a tea towel (dish towel).*

NUTRITION PER SERVE
Protein 13 g; Fat 25 g; Carbohydrate 1 g; Dietary Fibre 0 g; Cholesterol 30 mg; 1194 kJ (285 Cal)

Layer the bocconcini, basil and capsicum and then cover with the warmed oil.

Mushroom pâté with toast

PREPARATION TIME: 15 MINUTES + 5 HOURS REFRIGERATION + 10 MINUTES COOLING | TOTAL COOKING TIME: 20 MINUTES | MAKES 24

60 g (2¼ oz) butter
1 small onion, chopped
3 garlic cloves, crushed
375 g (13 oz) button mushrooms, quartered
125 g (4½ oz/1 cup) slivered almonds, toasted
2 tablespoons pouring (whipping) cream
2 tablespoons finely chopped thyme
3 tablespoons finely chopped flat-leaf (Italian) parsley
6 thick slices wholegrain or wholemeal (whole-wheat) bread

NUTRITION PER TOAST WITH PATE
Protein 2.5 g; Fat 5.5 g; Carbohydrate 3.5 g; Dietary Fibre 1.5 g; Cholesterol 7.5 mg; 310 kJ (75 cal)

1 Heat the butter in a large frying pan. Cook the onion and garlic over medium heat for 2 minutes, or until soft. Increase the heat, add the mushrooms and cook for 5 minutes, or until the mushrooms are soft and most of the liquid has evaporated. Leave to cool for 10 minutes.

2 Roughly chop the almonds in a food processor. Add the mushroom mixture and process until smooth. With the motor running, gradually pour in the cream. Stir in the herbs and season with salt and freshly ground black pepper. Spoon into two 250 ml (9 fl oz/1 cup) ramekins and smooth the surface. Cover and refrigerate for 4–5 hours to let the flavours develop.

3 To make the toasts, preheat the oven to 180°C (350°F/Gas 4). Toast one side of the bread under a hot grill (broiler) until golden. Remove the crusts and cut each slice into four triangles. Place on a large oven tray in single layer, toasted side down, and cook for 5–10 minutes, or until crisp. Serve immediately with the pâté.

Cook the onion, garlic and mushrooms until the mushrooms are soft.

Blend the almonds and mushroom mixture in a food processor until smooth.

Spoon the pâté into the ramekins and smooth the surface.

Tamari nut mix

PREPARATION TIME: 15 MINUTES | TOTAL COOKING TIME: 25 MINUTES | SERVES 10–12

250 g (9 oz) mixed nuts (almonds, Brazil nuts, peanuts, walnuts)
125 g (4½ oz) pepitas (pumpkin seeds) (see NOTE)
125 g (4½ oz) sunflower seeds
125 g (4½ oz) cashew nuts
125 g (4½ oz) macadamia nuts
125 ml (4 fl oz/½ cup) tamari

1 Preheat the oven to 140°C (275°F/Gas 1). Lightly grease two large baking trays.

2 Place the mixed nuts, pepitas, sunflower seeds, cashew nuts and macadamia nuts in a large bowl. Pour the tamari over the nuts and seeds and toss together well, coating them evenly in the tamari. Leave for 10 minutes.

3 Spread the nut and seed mixture evenly over the baking trays and bake for 20–25 minutes, or until dry roasted. Cool completely and store in an airtight container for up to 2 weeks.

NOTE: *Pepitas, peeled pumpkin seeds, are available at most supermarkets and health-food stores.*

STORAGE: *Once stored, the nuts may become soft. If they do, spread them out flat on a baking tray and bake in oven at 150°C (300°F/Gas 2) for 5–10 minutes.*

Stir the tamari through the nuts, pepitas and sunflower seeds.

Spread the nut mixture evenly over two lightly oiled baking trays.

NUTRITION PER SERVE (12)
Protein 11.5 g; Fat 36 g; Carbohydrate 4 g; Dietary Fibre 5 g; Cholesterol 0 mg; 1604 kJ (383 Cal)

Ashed herbed goat's cheese

PREPARATION TIME: 15 MINUTES + OVERNIGHT REFRIGERATION | TOTAL COOKING TIME: 20 MINUTES | SERVES 8

4 sprigs sage
4 sprigs rosemary
4 sprigs thyme
4 sprigs marjoram
4 x 100 g (3½ oz) goat's cheese rounds or logs

1 Place the sage, rosemary, thyme and marjoram in a small saucepan. Cover and dry-cook over medium heat for 20 minutes without removing the lid. Remove from the heat and leave, covered, for 5 minutes. The herbs will be blackened. Transfer to a food processor and finely chop.

2 Pat the goat's cheese dry with paper towels. Spread the ash out on a large plate. Roll the goat's cheese in the ashed herbs to coat evenly. Cover with plastic wrap and refrigerate overnight. Serve as part of a cheese or antipasto platter, or toss through a salad.

NUTRITION PER SERVE
Protein 10 g; Fat 16 g; Carbohydrate 0 g; Dietary Fibre 0 g; Cholesterol 50 mg; 775 kJ (185 Cal)

After the herbs have been dry-cooked they will be blackened.

Put the goat's cheese on paper towels and pat dry so that the ash will stick.

Roll the goat's cheeses in the blackened herbs before refrigerating overnight.

Grissini

PREPARATION TIME: 30 MINUTES + 1 HOUR 10 MINUTES STANDING | TOTAL COOKING TIME: 20 MINUTES | MAKES 24

7 g (¼ oz) sachet dried yeast
1 teaspoon sugar
500 g (1 lb 2 oz/4 cups) plain (all-purpose) flour
3 tablespoons olive oil
2 small handfuls chopped basil
4 garlic cloves, crushed
50 g (1¾ oz) parmesan cheese, grated
2 teaspoons sea salt flakes
2 tablespoons grated parmesan cheese, extra

NUTRITION PER GRISSINI
Protein 3.5 g; Fat 3.5 g; Carbohydrate 16 g; Dietary Fibre 1 g; Cholesterol 3 mg; 457 kJ (109 Cal)

1 Put the yeast, sugar and 310 ml (10 fl oz/ 1¼ cups) warm water in a small bowl and leave in a warm place for about 5–10 minutes, or until frothy. Sift the flour and 1 teaspoon of salt into a bowl and stir in the yeast and oil. Add more water if the dough is dry.

2 Gather the dough into a ball and turn out onto a lightly floured surface. Knead for 10 minutes, or until soft and elastic. Divide into two portions and flatten into rectangles. Put the basil and garlic on one portion and the parmesan on the other. Fold the dough to enclose the fillings, then knead for a few minutes to incorporate evenly.

3 Place the doughs into two lightly oiled bowls and cover with plastic wrap. Leave in a warm place for about 1 hour, or until doubled in volume. Preheat the oven to 230°C (450°F/ Gas 8) and lightly grease two large baking trays.

4 Punch down the doughs and knead each again for 1 minute. Divide each piece of dough into 12 portions, and roll each portion into a stick 30 cm (12 inches) long. Place on the baking trays and brush with water. Sprinkle the basil and garlic dough with the sea salt, and the cheese dough with the extra parmesan. Bake for 15 minutes, or until crisp and golden brown. Grissini can be kept in an airtight container for up to a week.

Punch down the dough with your fist to expel the air and then knead for a minute.

Flatten one portion of dough into a circle and put the basil and garlic on top.

Divide the dough into 12 portions and roll each one into a long stick.

Marinated feta

PREPARATION TIME: 10 MINUTES + 1 WEEK REFRIGERATION | TOTAL COOKING TIME: NIL | SERVES 6 (AS PART OF AN ANTIPASTO PLATTER)

350 g (12 oz) feta cheese
1 tablespoon dried oregano
1 teaspoon coriander seeds
125 g (4½ oz) sun-dried tomatoes in oil
4 small red chillies
3–4 sprigs rosemary
olive oil

1 Pat the feta dry with paper towels, and cut into 2 cm (¾ inch) cubes. Place in a bowl and sprinkle the oregano, coriander seeds and 1 tablespoon of freshly ground black pepper over the cheese.

2 Drain the sun-dried tomatoes over a bowl so that you catch all of the oil. Arrange the feta, chillies, rosemary and sun-dried tomatoes in a sterilised 750 ml (26 fl oz/3 cup) wide-necked jar with a clip-top lid. Cover with the reserved sun-dried tomato oil—you should have about 3 tablespoons—and top up with olive oil. Seal and refrigerate for 1 week (it will keep for 1–2 months in the fridge). Serve at room temperature.

NOTE: *To sterilise a storage jar, rinse with boiling water then place in a warm oven until completely dry. Do not use a tea towel (dish towel) to dry.*

NUTRITION PER SERVE
Protein 10 g; Fat 15 g; Carbohydrate 1 g; Dietary Fibre 0.5 g; Cholesterol 40 mg; 698 kJ (167 Cal)

Sprinkle the oregano, coriander seeds and pepper over the cubes of feta.

Drain the sun-dried tomatoes over a small bowl to catch all the oil.

Arrange the ingredients in the jar and pour in the sun-dried tomato oil. Top up with olive oil.

Roasted balsamic onions

PREPARATION TIME: 15 MINUTES + REFRIGERATION | TOTAL COOKING TIME: 90 MINUTES | SERVES 8 (AS PART OF AN ANTIPASTO PLATTER)

1 kg (2 lb 4 oz) pickling onions, unpeeled (see NOTE)
185 ml (6 fl oz/¾ cup) balsamic vinegar
2 tablespoons soft brown sugar
185 ml (6 fl oz/¾ cup) olive oil

1 Preheat the oven to 160°C (315°F/Gas 2–3). Place the unpeeled onions in a baking tin and roast for 1½ hours. Leave until cool enough to handle. Trim the stems from the onions and peel away the skin (the outer part of the root should come away but the onions will remain intact). Rinse a 1 litre (35 fl oz/4 cup) wide-necked jar with boiling water and dry in a warm oven (do not dry with a tea towel (dish towel)). Add the onions to the jar.

2 Put the vinegar and sugar in a small screw-top jar and stir to dissolve the sugar. Add the oil, seal the jar and shake vigorously—the mixture will be paler and may separate on standing.

3 Pour the vinegar mixture over the onions, seal, and turn upside down to coat. Marinate overnight in the fridge, turning occasionally. Return to room temperature and shake to combine the dressing before serving.

NOTE: *Pickling onions are very small and usually packed in 1 kg (2 lb 4 oz) bags. The ideal size is around 35 g (1¼ oz) each. The sizes in the bag will probably range from 20 g (¾ oz) up to 40 g (1¼ oz). The cooking time given is suitable for this range and there is no need to cook the larger ones for any longer. The marinating time given is a minimum—the onions may be marinated for up to 3 days in the refrigerator. The marinade may separate after a few hours, which is fine—simply stir occasionally.*

When cool, trim the stems from the onions and peel away the skin.

Pour the vinegar mixture over the onions, turning the jar to coat thoroughly.

NUTRITION PER SERVE
Protein 0.5 g; Fat 7.5 g; Carbohydrate 20 g; Dietary Fibre 2 g; Cholesterol 0 mg; 677 kJ (162 Cal)

Salt and pepper tofu puffs

PREPARATION TIME: 15 MINUTES | TOTAL COOKING TIME: 10 MINUTES | SERVES 4–6

2 x 190 g (6¾ oz) packets deep-fried tofu puffs
250 g (9 oz/2 cups) cornflour (cornstarch)
2 tablespoons salt
1 tablespoon white pepper
2 teaspoons caster (superfine) sugar
4 egg whites, lightly beaten
oil, for deep-frying (see NOTE)
125 ml (4 fl oz/½ cup) sweet chilli sauce
2 tablespoons lemon juice
lemon wedges, to serve

NUTRITION PER SERVE (6)
Protein 55 g; Fat 10 g; Carbohydrate 44 g; Dietary Fibre 1 g; Cholesterol 0 mg; 1135 kJ (270 Cal)

1 Cut the tofu puffs in half and pat dry with paper towels.

2 Mix the cornflour, salt, pepper and caster sugar in a large bowl.

3 Dip the tofu into the egg white in batches, then toss in the cornflour mixture, shaking off any excess.

4 Fill a deep, heavy-based saucepan or wok one-third full with oil and heat until a cube of bread dropped into the oil browns in 15 seconds. Cook the tofu in batches for 1–2 minutes, or until crisp. Drain well on paper towels.

5 Place the sweet chilli sauce and lemon juice in a bowl and mix together well. Serve immediately with the tofu puffs and lemon wedges.

NOTE: *It is best to use a good-quality peanut oil to deep-fry the tofu puffs—the flavour will be slightly nutty.*

Dip the tofu puffs in the egg white, then in the cornflour, shaking off any excess.

Deep-fry the tofu in batches until crisp, then remove with a slotted spoon.

Beetroot hummus

PREPARATION TIME: 15 MINUTES | TOTAL COOKING TIME: 40 MINUTES | SERVES 8

500 g (1 lb 2 oz) beetroot (beets), trimmed
4 tablespoons olive oil
1 large onion, chopped
1 tablespoon ground cumin
400 g (14 oz) tin chickpeas, drained and rinsed
1 tablespoon tahini
90 g (3¼ oz/⅓ cup) plain yoghurt
3 garlic cloves, crushed
3 tablespoons lemon juice
125 ml (4 fl oz/½ cup) vegetable stock

1 Scrub the beetroot well. Bring a large saucepan of water to the boil over high heat and cook the beetroot for 35–40 minutes, or until soft and cooked through. Drain and cool slightly before peeling.

2 Meanwhile, heat 1 tablespoon of the oil in a frying pan over medium heat and cook the onion for 2–3 minutes, or until soft. Add the cumin and cook for a further 1 minute, or until fragrant.

3 Chop the beetroot and place in a food processor or blender with the onion mixture, chickpeas, tahini, yoghurt, garlic, lemon juice and stock and process until smooth. With the motor running, add the remaining oil in a thin steady stream. Process until the mixture is thoroughly combined. Serve with Lebanese or Turkish bread.

NOTE: *Beetroot hummus can be a great accompaniment to a main meal or is delicious as part of a meze platter with bruschetta or crusty bread. Its vivid colour sparks up any table.*

VARIATION: *You can use 500 g (1 lb 2 oz) of any vegetable to make the hummus. Try carrot or pumpkin (winter squash).*

Cook the beetroot until soft, then drain and cool slightly before peeling off the skins.

Put all the hummus ingredients in a food processor and blend until smooth.

NUTRITION PER SERVE
Protein 5.5 g; Fat 13 g; Carbohydrate 13 g; Dietary Fibre 5 g; Cholesterol 1.5 mg; 792 kJ (190 Cal)

Vegetable shapes with crème fraîche and fried leek

PREPARATION TIME: 25 MINUTES | TOTAL COOKING TIME: 45 MINUTES | MAKES 35

2 x 425 g (15 oz) long thin orange sweet potatoes
5 beetroot (beets)
125 g (4½ oz/½ cup) crème fraîche
1 garlic clove, crushed
¼ teaspoon grated lime zest
oil, for deep-frying
2 leeks, cut lengthways into very fine slices

1 Bring two large saucepans of water to the boil over high heat and place the sweet potatoes in one saucepan and the beetroot in the other. Boil, covered, for 30–40 minutes, or until tender, adding more boiling water if it starts to evaporate. Drain separately and set aside until cool enough to touch. Remove the skins from the beetroot. Trim the ends from the beetroot and sweet potatoes and cut both into 1 cm (½ inch) slices. Using a biscuit cutter, cut the slices into shapes. Drain on paper towels.

2 Place the crème fraîche, garlic and lime zest in a bowl and mix together well. Refrigerate until ready to use.

3 Fill a deep, heavy-based saucepan one-third full of oil and heat until a cube of bread dropped into the oil browns in 10 seconds. Cook the leek in four batches for 30 seconds, or until golden brown and crisp. Drain on paper towels and season with salt.

4 Place a teaspoon of crème fraîche mixture on top of each vegetable shape and top with some fried leek.

HINT: *You can make the crème fraîche mixture and deep-fry the leek the day before and keep them in separate airtight containers. If the leek softens, place on a baking tray and crisp in a hot oven for 5 minutes.*

NUTRITION PER VEGETABLE SHAPE
Protein 1 g; Fat 2 g; Carbohydrate 5.5 g; Dietary Fibre 1 g; Cholesterol 2.5 mg; 180 kJ (43 Cal)

Using a biscuit cutter, cut the beetroot and sweet potato into shapes.

Deep-fry the leek in batches until golden brown and crisp.

Soups and starters

Cream of asparagus soup

PREPARATION TIME: 20 MINUTES | TOTAL COOKING TIME: 55 MINUTES | SERVES 4–6

1 kg (2 lb 4 oz) asparagus spears
30 g (1 oz) butter
1 onion, finely chopped
1 litre (35 fl oz/4 cups) vegetable stock
1 small handful basil leaves, chopped
1 teaspoon celery salt
250 ml (9 fl oz/1 cup) pouring (whipping) cream

NUTRITION PER SERVE (6)
Protein 6 g; Fat 22 g; Carbohydrate 5 g; Dietary Fibre 3 g; Cholesterol 70 mg; 990 kJ (237 Cal)

1 Break off the woody ends from the asparagus (hold both ends of the spear and bend it gently—the woody end will snap off and can be thrown away) and trim off the tips. Blanch the tips in boiling water for 1–2 minutes, refresh in cold water and set aside. Chop the asparagus stems into large pieces.

2 Melt the butter in a large saucepan and cook the onion for 3–4 minutes over low–medium heat, or until soft and golden. Add the chopped asparagus stems and cook for 1–2 minutes, stirring continuously.

3 Add the stock, basil and celery salt. Bring to the boil, reduce the heat and simmer, covered, for 30 minutes.

4 Check that the asparagus is well cooked and soft. If not, simmer for a further 10 minutes. Set aside and allow to cool slightly.

5 Pour into a food processor and process in batches until smooth. Then sieve into a clean saucepan. Return to the heat, pour in the cream and gently reheat. Do not allow the soup to boil. Season to taste with salt and white pepper. Add the asparagus tips and serve immediately.

HINT: *If you are not using home-made stock, always taste before adding seasoning to your soup—shop-bought stock can be very salty.*

The woody end from the asparagus spear will snap off when you bend the spear

Test whether the asparagus is well cooked by piercing it with a fork.

Vegetable soup

PREPARATION TIME: 20 MINUTES + OVERNIGHT SOAKING | TOTAL COOKING TIME: 1 HOUR | SERVES 6

105 g (3½ oz/½ cup) dried red kidney beans or borlotti beans
1 tablespoon olive oil
1 leek, halved lengthways and chopped
1 small onion, diced
2 carrots, chopped
2 celery stalks, chopped
1 large zucchini (courgette), chopped
1 tablespoon tomato paste (concentrated purée)
1 litre (35 fl oz/4 cups) vegetable stock
400 g (14 oz) pumpkin (winter squash), cubed
2 potatoes, cubed
3 tablespoons chopped flat-leaf (Italian) parsley

1 Put the beans in a large bowl, cover with cold water and soak overnight. Rinse, then transfer to a saucepan, cover with cold water and cook for 45 minutes, or until just tender. Drain.

2 Meanwhile, heat the oil in a large saucepan. Add the leek and onion and cook over medium heat for 2–3 minutes without browning, or until they start to soften. Add the carrot, celery and zucchini and cook for 3–4 minutes. Add the tomato paste and stir for a further 1 minute. Pour in the stock and 1.25 litres (44 fl oz/5 cups) water and bring to the boil. Reduce the heat to low and leave to simmer for 20 minutes.

3 Add the pumpkin, potato, parsley and red kidney beans and simmer for a further 20 minutes, or until the vegetables are tender and the beans are cooked. Season to taste. Serve immediately with crusty wholemeal (whole-wheat) or wholegrain bread.

HINT: *To save time, use a 420 g (15 oz) tin of red kidney beans. Rinse and drain well before use.*

Using a sharp knife, cut the flesh of the pumpkin into small cubes.

Add the vegetables and beans and simmer until the vegetables are tender.

NUTRITION PER SERVE
Protein 7.5 g; Fat 4 g; Carbohydrate 19 g; Dietary Fibre 7 g; Cholesterol 0 mg; 600 KJ (143 Cal)

Soba noodle soup

PREPARATION TIME: 15 MINUTES + 5 MINUTES STANDING | TOTAL COOKING TIME: 10 MINUTES | SERVES 4

250 g (9 oz) packet soba noodles
2 dried shiitake mushrooms
2 litres (70 fl oz/8 cups) vegetable stock
120 g (4¼ oz) snow peas (mangetouts), cut into thin strips
2 small carrots, cut into thin matchsticks
2 garlic cloves, finely chopped
6 spring onions (scallions), cut into 5 cm (2 inch) lengths and sliced lengthways
3 cm (1¼ inch) piece fresh ginger, cut into thin matchsticks
4 tablespoons soy sauce
3 tablespoons mirin or sake
90 g (3¼ oz/1 cup) bean sprouts, trimmed
fresh coriander (cilantro), to garnish

1 Cook the noodles according to the packet instructions. Drain.

2 Soak the mushrooms in 125 ml (4 fl oz/½ cup) boiling water until soft. Drain, reserving the liquid. Remove the stalks and finely slice the mushrooms.

3 Combine the vegetable stock, mushrooms, reserved liquid, snow peas, carrot, garlic, spring onion and ginger in a large saucepan. Bring slowly to the boil, then reduce the heat to low and simmer for 5 minutes, or until the vegetables are tender. Add the soy sauce, mirin and bean sprouts. Cook for a further 3 minutes.

4 Divide the noodles among four large serving bowls. Ladle the hot liquid and vegetables over the top and garnish with coriander.

Using a sharp knife, carefully cut the ginger into thin matchsticks.

After soaking the mushrooms, drain and finely slice them.

NUTRITION PER SERVE
Protein 13 g; Fat 1.5 g; Carbohydrate 30 g; Dietary Fibre 6 g; Cholesterol 11 mg; 1124 kJ (270 Cal)

French onion soup

PREPARATION TIME: 30 MINUTES | TOTAL COOKING TIME: 1 HOUR 30 MINUTES | SERVES 4

55 g (2 oz) butter
1 tablespoon olive oil
1 kg (2 lb 4 oz) onions, thinly sliced into rings
840 ml (28 fl oz) vegetable stock
125 ml (4 fl oz/½ cup) dry sherry
½ baguette
35 g (1 oz/⅓ cup) grated parmesan cheese
125 g (4½ oz/1 cup) finely grated cheddar or gruyère cheeses
chopped parsley, to serve

NUTRITION PER SERVE
Protein 17 g; Fat 27 g; Carbohydrate 19 g; Dietary Fibre 4 g; Cholesterol 65 mg; 1735 kJ (415 Cal)

1 Heat the butter and oil in a large saucepan, then add the onion and cook, stirring frequently, over low heat for 45 minutes, or until softened and golden brown. It is important not to rush this stage—cook the onion thoroughly so that it caramelises and the flavours develop.

2 Add the vegetable stock, sherry and 250 ml (9 fl oz/1 cup) water. Bring to the boil, then reduce the heat and simmer for 30 minutes. Season to taste.

3 Meanwhile, slice the bread into four thick slices and arrange them in a single layer under a hot grill (broiler). Toast one side, turn and sprinkle with parmesan, and toast until crisp and golden and the cheese has melted.

4 Put the bread slices into serving bowls. Ladle in the hot soup, sprinkle with the cheese and parsley and serve.

Using a large sharp knife, thinly slice the onions into rings.

Heat the oil and butter in a large saucepan and then add the onion.

Stir frequently over low heat until the onion is softened and golden brown.

Chilli, corn and red capsicum soup

PREPARATION TIME: 20 MINUTES | TOTAL COOKING TIME: 45 MINUTES | SERVES 4

1 coriander (cilantro) sprig
4 corn cobs
30 g (1 oz) butter
2 red capsicums (peppers), diced
1 small onion, finely chopped
1 small red chilli, finely chopped
1 tablespoon plain (all-purpose) flour
500 ml (17 fl oz/2 cups) vegetable stock
125 ml (4 fl oz/½ cup) pouring (whipping) cream

1 Trim the leaves off the coriander and finely chop the root and stems. Cut the kernels off the corn cobs.

2 Heat the butter in a large saucepan over medium heat. Add the corn kernels, capsicum, onion and chilli and stir to coat the vegetables in the butter. Cook, covered, over low heat, stirring occasionally, for 10 minutes, or until the vegetables are soft. Increase the heat to medium and add the coriander root and stem. Cook, stirring, for 30 seconds, or until fragrant. Sprinkle with the flour and stir for a further minute. Remove from the heat and gradually add the vegetable stock, stirring together. Add 500 ml (17 fl oz/2 cups) water and return to the heat. Bring to the boil, reduce the heat to low and simmer, covered, for 30 minutes, or until the vegetables are tender. Cool slightly.

3 Ladle about 500 ml (17 fl oz/2 cups) of the soup into a blender and purée until smooth. Return the purée to the soup in the saucepan, pour in the cream and gently heat until warmed through. Season to taste with salt. Sprinkle with the coriander leaves to serve. Delicious with grilled (broiled) cheese on pitta bread.

Using a sharp knife, cut all the kernels from the corn cob.

Trim the leaves and finely chop the root and stems of the coriander.

NUTRITION PER SERVE
Protein 5.5 g; Fat 20 g; Carbohydrate 24 g; Dietary Fibre 4 g; Cholesterol 62 mg; 1269 kJ (303 Cal)

Chickpea and herb dumpling soup

PREPARATION TIME: 30 MINUTES | TOTAL COOKING TIME: 35 MINUTES | SERVES 4

1 tablespoon oil
1 onion, chopped
2 garlic cloves, crushed
2 teaspoons ground cumin
1 teaspoon ground coriander
¼ teaspoon chilli powder
2 x 300 g (10½ oz) tins chickpeas
875 ml (30 fl oz/3½ cups) vegetable stock
2 x 425 g (15 oz) tins chopped tomatoes
1 tablespoon chopped fresh coriander (cilantro) leaves
125 g (4½ oz/1 cup) self-raising flour
30 g (1 oz) butter, chopped
2 tablespoons grated parmesan cheese
2 tablespoons mixed chopped herbs (chives, parsley, coriander)
3 tablespoons milk

1 Heat the oil in a large saucepan, and cook the onion over medium heat for 2–3 minutes, or until soft. Add the garlic, cumin, ground coriander and chilli and cook for 1 minute, or until fragrant. Add the chickpeas, stock and tomato. Bring to the boil, then reduce the heat and simmer, covered, for 10 minutes. Stir in the coriander.

2 To make the dumplings, sift the flour into a bowl and add the chopped butter. Rub together with your fingertips until the mixture resembles fine breadcrumbs. Stir in the parmesan and herbs. Make a well in the centre, add the milk and mix with a flat-bladed knife until just combined. Bring together into a rough ball, divide into eight portions and roll into small balls.

3 Add the dumplings to the soup, cover and simmer for 20 minutes, or until a skewer comes out clean when inserted into the centre of a dumpling.

NUTRITION PER SERVE
Protein 17 g; Fat 16 g; Carbohydrate 50 g; Dietary Fibre 12 g; Cholesterol 23 mg; 1767 kJ (422 Cal)

Add the milk to the dumpling mixture and mix with a flat-bladed knife.

Pierce the dumplings with a skewer to test if they are cooked.

Carrot timbales with creamy saffron and leek sauce

PREPARATION TIME: 25 MINUTES | TOTAL COOKING TIME: 1 HOUR | SERVES 6 AS A STARTER

60 g (2¼ oz) butter
2 leeks, sliced
2 garlic cloves, crushed
1 kg (2 lb 4 oz) carrots, sliced
375 ml (13 fl oz/1½ cups) vegetable stock
1½ tablespoons finely chopped sage
3 tablespoons pouring (whipping) cream
4 eggs, lightly beaten

CREAMY SAFFRON AND LEEK SAUCE
40 g (1½ oz) butter
1 small leek, finely sliced
1 large garlic clove, crushed
3 tablespoons dry white wine
pinch of saffron threads
90 g (3¼ oz/⅓ cup) crème fraîche

NUTRITION PER SERVE
Protein 7 g; Fat 25 g; Carbohydrate 11 g; Dietary Fibre 6 g; Cholesterol 187 mg; 1258 kJ (300 Cal)

1 Preheat the oven to 170°C (325°F/Gas 3). Lightly grease six 185 ml (6 fl oz/¾ cup) timbale moulds. Heat the butter in a saucepan and cook the leek for 3–4 minutes, or until soft. Add garlic and carrot and cook for a further 2–3 minutes. Pour in the stock and 500 ml (17 fl oz/2 cups) water, bring to the boil. Reduce the heat. Simmer, covered, for 5 minutes, or until the carrot is tender. Strain, reserving 185 ml (6 fl oz/¾ cup) of the liquid.

2 Blend the carrot mixture, 125 ml (4 fl oz/½ cup) of the reserved liquid and the sage in a food processor until smooth. Cool the mixture and stir in cream and egg. Season and pour into the moulds. Place moulds in roasting tin filled with hot water halfway up their sides. Bake for 30–40 minutes, or until just set.

3 To make sauce, melt the butter in a saucepan and cook the leek for 3–4 minutes without browning. Add the garlic and cook for 30 seconds. Add the wine, reserved liquid and saffron. Bring to the boil. Reduce the heat and simmer for 5 minutes, or until reduced. Stir in the crème fraîche.

4 Turn out the timbales onto serving plates and serve with the sauce.

Pour the mixture into the prepared moulds and place in a roasting tin.

Cook the leek, garlic, wine, reserved liquid and saffron on low heat until reduced.

Carefully turn out the carrot timbales onto serving plates.

Gazpacho

PREPARATION TIME: 40 MINUTES + 3 HOURS REFRIGERATION | TOTAL COOKING TIME: NIL | SERVES 4–6

750 g (1 lb 10 oz) ripe tomatoes
1 Lebanese (short) cucumber, chopped
1 green capsicum (pepper), chopped
2–3 garlic cloves, crushed
1–2 tablespoons finely chopped black olives
4 tablespoons red or white wine vinegar
3 tablespoons olive oil
1 tablespoon tomato paste (concentrated purée)

ACCOMPANIMENTS
1 onion, finely chopped
1 red capsicum (pepper), finely chopped
2 spring onions (scallions), finely chopped
1 Lebanese (short) cucumber, finely chopped
2 hard-boiled eggs, chopped
1 small handful mint or parsley, chopped
croutons

1 To peel the tomatoes, score a cross in the base of each tomato. Cover with boiling water for 30 seconds, then plunge into cold water. Drain and peel away the tomato skin from the cross. Chop the flesh so finely that it is almost a purée.

2 Mix together the tomato, cucumber, capsicum, garlic, olives, vinegar, oil and tomato paste, and season to taste with salt and freshly ground black pepper. Cover and refrigerate for 2–3 hours.

3 Use 750 ml (26 fl oz/3 cups) chilled water to thin the soup to your taste. Serve chilled, with the chopped onion, capsicum, spring onion, cucumber, boiled egg, herbs and croutons served separately for diners to add to their own bowls.

Halve the cucumber lengthways, cut into strips and chop finely.

Using a sharp knife, chop the tomato flesh very finely to a purée.

NUTRITION PER SERVE (6)
Protein 5 g; Fat 2 g; Carbohydrate 7 g; Dietary Fibre 4 g; Cholesterol 70 mg; 310 kJ (75 Cal)

Lentil and spinach soup

PREPARATION TIME: 25 MINUTES | TOTAL COOKING TIME: 1 HOUR | SERVES 8

95 g (3¼ oz/½ cup) brown lentils
2 tablespoons vegetable oil
1 leek, chopped
1 onion, chopped
1 celery stalk, chopped
600 g (1 lb 5 oz) potatoes, chopped
1 litre (35 fl oz/4 cups) vegetable stock
250 g (9 oz) English spinach

1 Put the lentils in a saucepan. Cover with water and bring to the boil, reduce the heat and simmer for 20 minutes, or until tender. Drain.

2 Heat the oil in a large saucepan. Cook the leek, onion and celery for 5 minutes, or until softened. Add the potato and cook, stirring frequently, for 10 minutes. Add the vegetable stock and bring to the boil. Reduce the heat and simmer, covered, for 20 minutes, or until the potato is tender.

3 Remove the stalks from the spinach, wash the leaves well, add to the soup and cook for 1–2 minutes. Let the soup cool for a couple of minutes, then purée in a food processor or blender. Return to the pan, add the lentils and reheat gently before serving.

NUTRITION PER SERVE
Protein 5 g; Fat 5 g; Carbohydrate 15 g; Dietary Fibre 4 g; Cholesterol 0 mg; 505 kJ (120 Cal)

Place the lentils in a saucepan and cover with plenty of cold water.

Cook the leek, onion and celery until soft, then add the chopped potato.

Add the cooked and drained lentils to the puréed soup in the pan.

Blue cheese gnocchi

PREPARATION TIME: 20 MINUTES | TOTAL COOKING TIME: 20 MINUTES | SERVES 8 AS A STARTER

500 g (1 lb 2 oz) potatoes, quartered
155 g (5½ oz/1¼ cups) plain (all-purpose) flour

SAUCE
300 ml (10½ fl oz) pouring (whipping) cream
125 g (4½ oz) gorgonzola cheese, roughly chopped
2 tablespoons snippped chives

NUTRITION PER SERVE
Protein 10 g; Fat 22 g; Carbohydrate 22 g; Dietary Fibre 1.5 g; Cholesterol 65 mg; 1370 kJ (325 Cal)

1 Cook the potatoes in boiling salted water for 15–20 minutes, or in the microwave until tender. Stir through a generous amount of salt. Drain the potatoes, then mash until completely smooth. Transfer to a bowl.

2 Sprinkle the flour into the bowl with one hand while kneading it into the potato mixture with the other hand. Continue kneading until all the flour is worked in and the dough is smooth. This should take a few minutes and will be sticky at first.

3 Divide the dough into three and roll each portion into a sausage that is 2 cm (¾ inch) thick. Cut into 2.5 cm (1 inch) lengths and, using floured hands, press each gnocchi against a fork to flatten it and indent one side (the indentation helps the sauce coat the gnocchi).

4 Bring a large saucepan of water to the boil. Drop in the gnocchi, then reduce the heat and simmer until they rise to the surface. This will take 2–3 minutes. Lift out of the water with a slotted spoon and drain well. Arrange on a warm serving dish and keep warm.

5 Put the cream into a small saucepan and bring to the boil. Boil rapidly, stirring constantly, for about 5 minutes, or until reduced by one third. Remove from the heat and stir in the cheese. Season with salt and freshly ground black pepper, and pour over the gnocchi. Scatter the chives over the top and serve immediately.

Add the flour with one hand while kneading it into the potato with the other.

Gently knead the mixture until all the flour is mixed in and the dough is smooth.

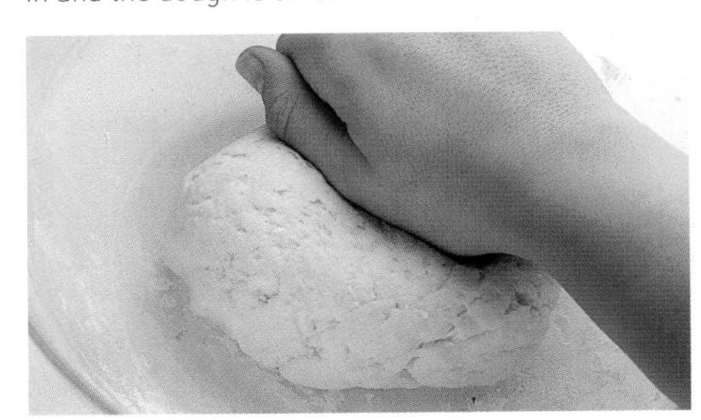

Press the gnocchi against a fork to flatten it and indent one side.

Roast pumpkin soup

PREPARATION TIME: 20 MINUTES | TOTAL COOKING TIME: 55 MINUTES | SERVES 6

1.25 kg (2 lb 12 oz) pumpkin (winter squash), peeled and cut into chunks
2 tablespoons olive oil
1 large onion, chopped
2 teaspoons ground cumin
1 large carrot, chopped
1 celery stalk, chopped
1 litre (35 fl oz/4 cups) vegetable stock
sour cream, to serve
finely chopped parsley, to serve
ground nutmeg, to serve

1 Preheat the oven to 180°C (350°F/Gas 4). Put the pumpkin on a greased baking tray and lightly brush with half the olive oil. Bake for 25 minutes, or until softened and slightly browned around the edges.

2 Heat the remaining oil in a large saucepan. Cook the onion and cumin for 2 minutes, then add the carrot and celery and cook for 3 minutes more, stirring frequently. Add the roasted pumpkin and stock. Bring to the boil, then reduce the heat and simmer for 20 minutes.

3 Allow to cool a little then purée in batches in a blender or food processor. Return the soup to the pan and gently reheat without boiling. Season to taste with salt and freshly ground black pepper. Top with sour cream and sprinkle with chopped parsley and ground nutmeg before serving.

NOTE: *Butternut pumpkin is often used in soups as it has a sweeter flavour than other varieties.*

HINT: *If the soup is too thick, thin it down with a little more stock.*

Lightly brush the pumpkin chunks with oil and bake until softened.

Transfer the cooled mixture to a blender or food processor and purée in batches.

NUTRITION PER SERVE
Protein 5 g; Fat 8.5 g; Carbohydrate 15 g; Dietary Fibre 3.5 g; Cholesterol 4.5 mg; 665 kJ (160 Cal)

Eggplant and coriander tostadas

PREPARATION TIME: 20 MINUTES | TOTAL COOKING TIME: 30 MINUTES | SERVES 4 AS A STARTER

1 small eggplant (aubergine), cut into cubes
½ red capsicum (pepper), cut into squares
½ red onion, cut into thin wedges
2 tablespoons olive oil
1 large garlic clove, crushed
1 small loaf wood-fired bread, cut into 12 slices
1 small ripe tomato, halved
2 tablespoons chopped mint
2 tablespoons chopped coriander (cilantro) roots, stems and leaves
60 g (2¼ oz) slivered almonds, toasted

1 Preheat the oven to 240°C (475°F/Gas 9). Put the eggplant, capsicum, onion and oil in a large bowl and mix to coat with the oil. Spread out in a single layer in a large roasting tin. Bake for 15 minutes, then turn the vegetables over and bake for a further 10 minutes, or until tender. Transfer to a bowl, add the garlic and season to taste with salt and freshly ground black pepper.

2 Place the bread on a baking tray and bake for 4 minutes, or until crisp. Rub the cut side of the tomato onto one side of each bread slice, squeezing the tomato to get as much liquid as possible. Then finely chop he tomato flesh and add to the vegetables with the mint and coriander.

3 Spoon the vegetables onto the tomato side of the bread and sprinkle with the almonds. Serve immediately.

NOTE: *You can roast the vegetables and toast the almonds up to a day ahead. Store in an airtight container.*

Spread the oil-coated vegetables in a single layer in a large roasting tin.

Rub the cut side of the tomato onto one side of each slice of bread.

NUTRITION PER SERVE
Protein 10 g; Fat 18 g; Carbohydrate 34 g; Dietary Fibre 5 g; Cholesterol 0 mg; 1415 kJ (340 Cal)

Individual vegetable terrines with spicy tomato sauce

PREPARATION TIME: 40 MINUTES | TOTAL COOKING TIME: 50 MINUTES | SERVES 4 AS A STARTER

125 ml (4 fl oz/½ cup) oil
1 red capsicum (pepper), grilled (broiled) peeled and cut into large pieces
1 yellow capsicum grilled (broiled), peeled and cut into large pieces
500 g (1 lb 2 oz) eggplant (aubergine), sliced
2 zucchini (courgettes), sliced on the diagonal
1 small fennel bulb, sliced
1 red onion, sliced
300 g (10½ oz) ricotta cheese
60 g (2¼ oz) grated parmesan cheese
1 tablespoon chopped flat-leaf (Italian) parsley
1 tablespoon snipped chives

SPICY TOMATO SAUCE
1 tablespoon oil
1 onion, finely chopped
2 garlic cloves, crushed
1 red chilli, seeded and chopped
425 g (15 oz) tin chopped tomatoes
2 tablespoons tomato paste (concentrated purée)

1 Heat 1 tablespoon of the oil in a large frying pan. Cook the vegetables in separate batches over high heat for 5 minutes, or until golden, adding the remaining oil as needed. Drain each vegetable separately on paper towels.

2 Preheat the oven to 200°C (400°F/Gas 6). Place the cheeses and herbs in a small bowl and mix together well. Season to taste.

3 Lightly grease four 310 ml (10¾ fl oz/ 1¼ cup) ramekins and line with baking paper. Using half the eggplant, put a layer in the base of each dish. Layer the capsicum, zucchini, cheese mixture, fennel and onion over the eggplant. Cover with the remaining eggplant and press down firmly. Bake for 10–15 minutes, or until hot. Leave for 5 minutes before turning out.

4 To make the sauce, heat the oil in a saucepan and cook the onion and garlic for 2–3 minutes, or until soft. Add the chilli, tomato and tomato paste and simmer for 5 minutes, or until thick and pulpy. Purée in a food processor. Return to the saucepan and keep warm. Spoon over the terrines.

NUTRITION PER SERVE
Protein 18 g; Fat 48 g; Carbohydrate 16 g; Dietary Fibre 8.5 g; Cholesterol 48 mg; 2346 kJ (560 Cal)

Cook the capsicums under a hot grill until blackened. Cool, peel, then cut into pieces.

Layer the fennel over the cheese mixture, then add a layer of onion.

Simmer the tomato sauce for 5 minutes, or until thick and pulpy.

Pies and pastries

Vegetable, feta and pesto parcels

PREPARATION TIME: 40 MINUTES | TOTAL COOKING TIME: 30 MINUTES | SERVES 4

30 g (1 oz) butter
2 garlic cloves, crushed
150 g (5½ oz) asparagus spears, trimmed and chopped
1 carrot, cut into thin matchsticks
1 zucchini (courgette), cut into thin matchsticks
1 red capsicum (pepper), cut into thin matchsticks
6 spring onions (scallions), thinly sliced on the diagonal
90 g (3¼ oz) mild feta cheese, crumbled
8 sheets filo pastry
60 g (2¼ oz) butter, melted
90 g (3¼ oz/⅓ cup) good-quality ready-made pesto
2 teaspoons sesame seed
tomato chutney, to serve

1 Preheat the oven to 200°C (400°F/Gas 6). Heat the butter in a large frying pan, then add the garlic and vegetables. Cook over medium heat for 3–4 minutes, or until just tender. Cool completely and fold in the feta. Divide the mixture into four equal portions.

2 Work with four sheets of pastry at a time, keeping the rest covered with a damp tea towel (dish towel). Brush each sheet with melted butter and lay them on top of one another. Cut in half widthways and spread 1 tablespoon of the pesto in the centre of each half, leaving a 2 cm (1 inch) border lengthways. Place one portion of the vegetable feta mixture on top of the pesto. Repeat the process with the remaining pastry, pesto and filling.

3 Brush the edges of filo with a little butter, tuck in the sides and fold over the ends to make four parcels. Place on a greased baking tray, seam side down, brush with the remaining butter and sprinkle with sesame seeds. Bake for 20–25 minutes, or until golden. Cut in half diagonally and serve hot with tomato chutney.

NUTRITION PER SERVE
Protein 28 g; Fat 16 g; Carbohydrate 126 g; Dietary Fibre 6 g; Cholesterol 30 mg; 3205 kJ (766 Cal)

With a sharp knife, slice the carrot and zucchini thinly into matchsticks.

Cover the pesto with one portion of the vegetable feta mixture.

Tuck in the sides and roll up the parcel until it sits on the unsecured end.

Artichoke and provolone quiches

PREPARATION TIME: 40 MINUTES + 30 MINUTES REFRIGERATION | TOTAL COOKING TIME: 35 MINUTES | SERVES 4

250 g (9 oz/2 cups) plain (all-purpose) flour
125 g (4½ oz) cold butter, chopped
1 egg yolk

FILLING
1 small eggplant (aubergine), sliced
1 tablespoon olive oil
6 eggs, lightly beaten
3 teaspoons wholegrain mustard
150 g (5½ oz) provolone cheese, grated
200 g (7 oz) marinated artichokes, sliced
125 g (4½ oz) semi-dried (sun-blushed) tomatoes

1 Process the flour and butter in a processor for about 15 seconds until crumbly. Add the egg yolk and 3 tablespoons of water. Process in short bursts until the mixture comes together. Add a little extra water if you think the dough is a bit too dry. Turn out onto a floured surface and gather into a ball. Cover with plastic wrap and refrigerate for at least 30 minutes.

2 Preheat the oven to 190°C (375°F/Gas 5) and grease four 11 cm (4¼ inch) oval pie tins.

3 To make the filling, brush the sliced eggplant with olive oil and place under a grill (broiler) until golden. Combine the eggs, mustard and cheese in a bowl.

4 Roll out the pastry and line the tins. Trim away the excess pastry and decorate the edges. Place one eggplant slice and a few artichokes and tomatoes in each tin, pour the egg mixture over the top and bake for 25 minutes, or until golden.

Brush each slice of eggplant with a little olive oil and then grill until golden.

Place one slice of eggplant in the bottom of each lined pie tin.

NUTRITION PER QUICHE
Protein 29.9 g; Fat 51.2 g; Carbohydrate 48.7 g; Dietary Fibre 5.3 g; Cholesterol 431 mg; 3277 kJ (783 Cal)

Mushroom and ricotta filo tart

PREPARATION TIME: 35 MINUTES | TOTAL COOKING TIME: 40 MINUTES | SERVES 6

60 g (2¼ oz) butter
270 g (9½ oz) field mushrooms, sliced
2 garlic cloves, crushed
1 tablespoon dry marsala
1 teaspoon thyme leaves
½ teaspoon chopped rosemary leaves
pinch of freshly grated nutmeg
5 sheets filo pastry
70 g (2½ oz) butter, extra, melted
200 g (7 oz) ricotta cheese
2 eggs, lightly beaten
125 ml (4 fl oz/½ cup) sour cream
1 tablespoon chopped parsley

1 Preheat the oven to 180°C (350°F/Gas 4). Melt the butter in a frying pan and add the mushrooms. Cook over high heat for a few minutes, until they begin to soften. Add the garlic and cook for another minute. Stir in the marsala, thyme, rosemary and nutmeg. Remove the mushrooms from the pan, carefully draining off any liquid.

2 Work with one sheet of filo pastry at a time, keeping the rest covered with a damp tea towel (dish towel) to stop them drying out. Brush the sheets with melted butter and fold in half. Place on top of each other to line a shallow 23 cm (9 inch) loose-based fluted flan (tart) tin, allowing the edges to overhang.

3 Beat the ricotta, eggs and sour cream together and season to taste. Spoon half the mixture into the tin, then add the mushrooms. Top with the rest of the ricotta mixture. Bake for 35 minutes, or until firm. Sprinkle with the chopped parsley to serve.

Brush the filo with melted butter, fold in half and layer into the tin.

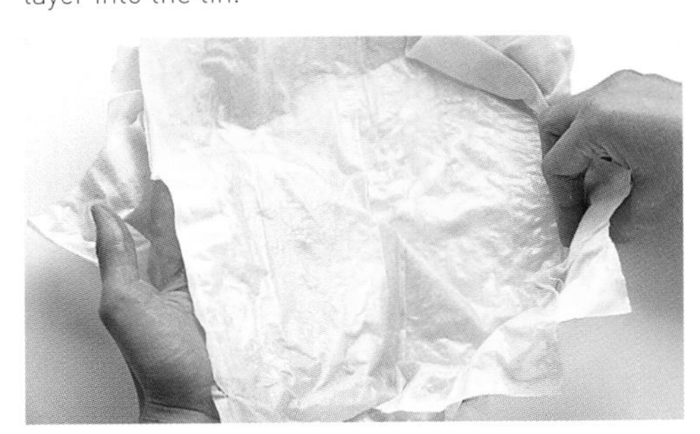

Layer half the ricotta filling into the pastry, then spread the mushrooms over the top.

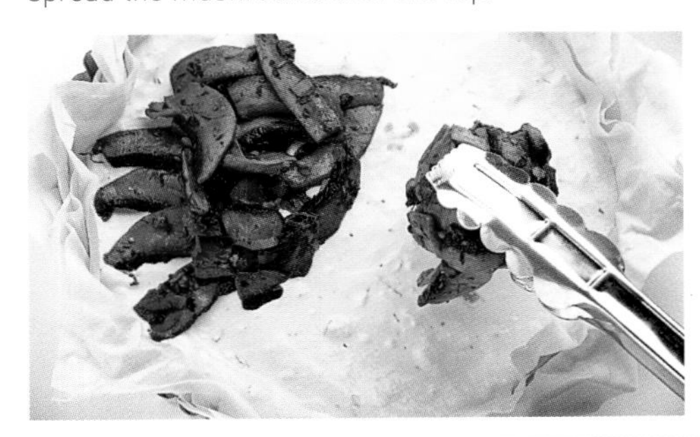

NUTRITION PER SERVE
Protein 9 g; Fat 35 g; Carbohydrate 9 g; Dietary Fibre 2 g; Cholesterol 160 mg; 1515 kJ (360 Cal)

Tomato and goat's cheese pie

PREPARATION TIME: 30 MINUTES + 20 MINUTES REFRIGERATION | TOTAL COOKING TIME: 30 MINUTES | SERVES 6

185 g (6½ oz/1½ cups) plain (all-purpose) flour
100 g (3½ oz) cold butter, chopped
3 tablespoons grated mature cheddar cheese

FILLING
1 egg yolk, lightly beaten
3 tablespoons dried breadcrumbs
4–5 tomatoes, sliced
100 g (3½ oz) goat's cheese
1 tablespoon olive oil
2 tablespoons small basil leaves or shredded basil, to serve

NUTRITION PER SERVE
Protein 10 g; Fat 25 g; Carbohydrate 30 g; Dietary Fibre 3 g; Cholesterol 95 mg; 1620 kJ (385 Cal)

1 Place the flour and butter in a food processor and process until crumbly. Add the cheddar, ½ teaspoon of salt and 2–3 tablespoons of water. Process in short bursts until the mixture just comes together, adding a little extra water if necessary. Turn the mixture out onto a floured surface and quickly bring it together into a ball. Cover the pastry with plastic wrap and refrigerate for at least 20 minutes.

2 Preheat the oven to 180°C (350°F/Gas 4). Roll out the pastry on a lightly floured surface into a circle about 35 cm (14 inches) in diameter. Wrap the pastry around a rolling pin and carefully lift it onto a greased baking tray. Carefully unroll the pastry into the tray.

3 Brush most of the egg yolk lightly over the pastry and sprinkle with the breadcrumbs. Arrange the slices of tomato on the pastry so that they overlap in a circle leaving a wide border. Crumble the goat's cheese over the top of the tomatoes. Turn the edge of the pastry in over the tomato filling and brush with the remaining egg yolk (mix with a little milk if there's not much egg left).

4 Bake for 30 minutes, or until the pastry is golden and the cheese has melted. Then drizzle with the olive oil and season well with salt and freshly ground black pepper. Scatter the top of the pie with the basil leaves to serve.

Process the flour and butter until crumbly, then add the cheese.

Lay the slices of tomato on the pastry and breadcrumbs so that they overlap.

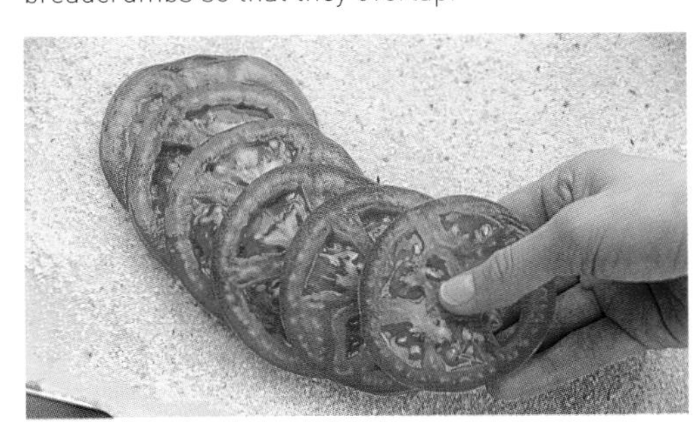

Turn in the pastry edge over the tomato and goat's cheese filling.

Cheese 'n' tattie pie

PREPARATION TIME: 45 MINUTES | TOTAL COOKING TIME: 40 MINUTES | SERVES 6–8

1 kg (2 lb 4 oz) new potatoes, unpeeled, cooked and sliced
125 g (4½ oz/1 cup) grated cheddar cheese
1 garlic clove, crushed
2 tablespoons snipped chives
2 tablespoons chopped marjoram
4 tablespoons whipped cream
2 eggs
2 sheets ready-rolled puff pastry
1 egg yolk, beaten, to glaze

1 Preheat the oven to 220°C (425°F/Gas 7). Place half the potatoes, overlapping the slices, in the base of a large round dish, and season generously with salt and freshly ground black pepper. Sprinkle with half the cheese, garlic, chives and marjoram. Top with another layer of potato, cheese, garlic, chives and marjoram.

2 Mix together the cream and eggs and pour over the potato.

3 Cut each pastry sheet into quarters, and each quarter into three equal lengths. Place the strips, overlapping, around the top of the pie, leaving the centre open. Press down the edges so that the pastry sticks to the pie dish, then trim the edge. Combine the egg yolk with a little water and brush the top of the pie.

4 Bake for 15 minutes; reduce the heat to 180°C (350°F/Gas 4), and bake for a further 15–20 minutes, or until the pastry is puffed and golden and the filling is set. Leave to stand for 10 minutes before serving.

Top with another layer of potato slices, cheese, garlic, chives and marjoram.

Overlap the pastry strips around the top of the pie, leaving the centre open.

NUTRITION PER SERVE (8)
Protein 15 g; Fat 20 g; Carbohydrate 30 g; Dietary Fibre 3 g; Cholesterol 115 mg; 1620 kJ (385 Cal)

Borekas

PREPARATION TIME: 30 MINUTES | TOTAL COOKING TIME: 20 MINUTES | MAKES 24

225 g (8 oz) feta cheese, crumbled
200 g (7 oz) cream cheese, slightly softened
2 eggs, lightly beaten
¼ teaspoon ground nutmeg
20 sheets filo pastry
60 g (2¼ oz) butter, melted
3 tablespoons sesame seeds

1 Preheat the oven to 180°C (350°F/Gas 4). Place the feta, cream cheese, egg and nutmeg in a bowl and mix until just combined—the mixture will be lumpy.

2 Work with five sheets of pastry at a time, keeping the rest covered with a damp tea towel (dish towel). Lay each sheet on a work surface, brush with melted butter and lay them on top of each other. Use a ruler as guidance to cut the filo into six equal strips.

3 Place 1 tablespoon of the filling at one end of a strip, leaving a narrow border. Fold the pastry over to enclose the filling and form a triangle. Continue folding the triangle over until you reach the end of the pastry, tucking any excess pastry under. Repeat with the remaining ingredients to make 24 triangles, and place on a lined baking tray.

4 Lightly brush with the remaining melted butter and sprinkle with sesame seeds. Bake for 15–20 minutes, or until puffed and golden.

NUTRITION PER BOREKA
Protein 4.5 g; Fat 8.5 g; Carbohydrate 6.5 g; Dietary Fibre 0.5 g; Cholesterol 35 mg; 505 kJ (120 Cal)

Using a straight edge for guidance, cut the filo sheets into six even strips.

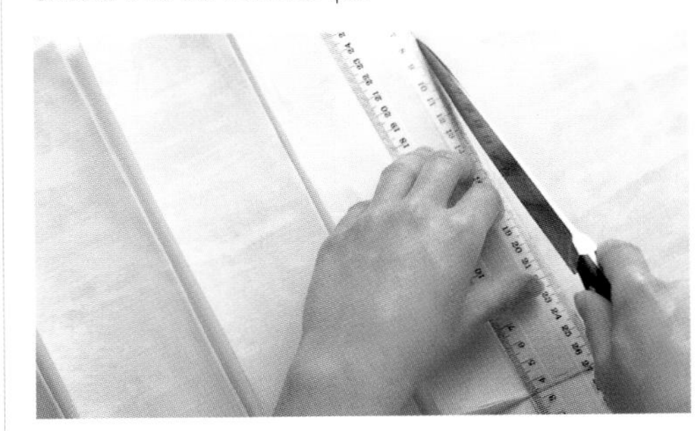

Fold the pastry over the filling, then continue folding until the end.

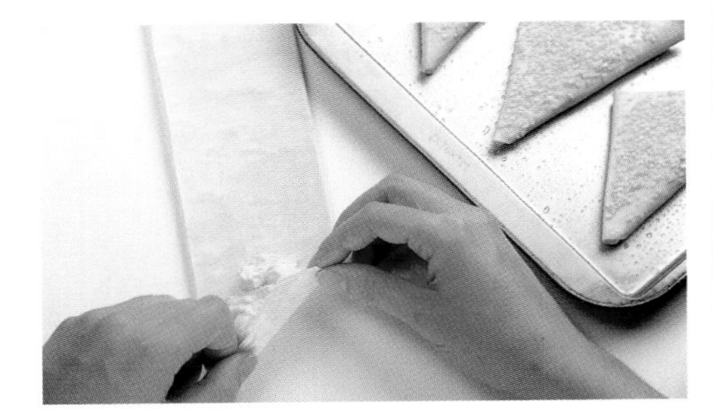

Sweet potato and lentil pastry pouches

PREPARATION TIME: 45 MINUTES | TOTAL COOKING TIME: 55 MINUTES | MAKES 32

- 2 tablespoons olive oil
- 1 large leek, finely chopped
- 2 garlic cloves, crushed
- 125 g (4½ oz) button mushrooms, roughly chopped
- 2 teaspoons ground cumin
- 2 teaspoons ground coriander
- 95 g (3¼ oz/½ cup) brown or green lentils
- 125 g (4½ oz/½ cup) red lentils
- 500 ml (17 fl oz/2 cups) vegetable stock
- 300 g (10½ oz) sweet potato, cubed
- 4 tablespoons finely chopped coriander (cilantro) leaves
- 8 sheets ready-rolled puff pastry
- 1 egg, lightly beaten
- ½ leek, extra, cut into long thin strips
- 200 g (7 oz) plain yoghurt
- 2 tablespoons grated Lebanese (short) cucumber
- ½ teaspoon soft brown sugar

NUTRITION PER PASTRY POUCH
Protein 5 g; Fat 11 g; Carbohydrate 20 g; Dietary Fibre 2 g; Cholesterol 17 mg; 835 kJ (200 Cal)

1 Preheat the oven to 200°C (400°F/Gas 6). Heat the oil in a saucepan over medium heat and cook the leek for 2–3 minutes, or until soft. Add the garlic, mushrooms, cumin and ground coriander and cook for 1 minute, or until fragrant.

2 Add the combined lentils and stock and bring to the boil. Reduce the heat and simmer for 20–25 minutes, or until the lentils are cooked through, stirring occasionally. Add the sweet potato in the last 5 minutes.

3 Transfer to a bowl and stir in the fresh coriander. Season to taste. Cool.

4 Cut the pastry sheets into four even squares. Place 1½ tablespoons of the filling into the centre of each pastry square and bring the edges together to form a pouch. Pinch together, then tie each pouch with string. Lightly brush with egg and place on lined baking trays. Bake for 20–25 minutes, or until the pastry is puffed and golden.

5 Soak the leek strips in boiling water for 30 seconds. Remove the string and re-tie with a piece of blanched leek. Put the yoghurt, cucumber and sugar in a bowl and mix together well. Serve with the pastry pouches.

Stir the coriander leaves into the cooked lentils and sweet potato.

Put the filling in the centre of each square, form a pouch and tie with string.

Blanch the long strips of leek by soaking them for 30 seconds in boiling water.

Blue cheese and onion flan

PREPARATION TIME: 40 MINUTES + 20 MINUTES REFRIGERATION | TOTAL COOKING TIME: 1 HOUR 40 MINUTES | SERVES 8

2 tablespoons olive oil
1 kg (2 lb 4 oz) red onions, very thinly sliced
1 teaspoon soft brown sugar
250 g (9 oz/2 cups) plain (all-purpose) flour
100 g (3½ oz) cold butter, cubed
185 ml (6 fl oz/¾ cup) pouring (whipping) cream
3 eggs
100 g (3½ oz) blue cheese, crumbled
1 teaspoon freshly chopped lemon thyme or thyme leaves

1 Heat the oil in a heavy-based frying pan over low heat. Add the onion and sugar and cook, stirring regularly, for 4–5 minutes, or until the onion is soft and lightly golden.

2 Process the flour and butter in a food processor for 15 seconds. Add 1–2 tablespoons of iced water and process in short bursts until the mixture just comes together. Turn out onto a floured surface and gather into a ball. Cover with plastic wrap and refrigerate for 10 minutes.

3 Preheat the oven to 180°C (350°F/Gas 4). Roll out the pastry thinly on a lightly floured surface to fit a greased 22 cm (8½ inch) round fluted loose-based flan (tart) tin. Trim any excess pastry. Chill for 10 minutes. Line with crumpled baking paper and fill with baking beads or rice. Put on a baking tray and bake for 10 minutes. Remove the paper and beads, then bake for a further 10 minutes, or until lightly golden and dry to the touch.

4 Cool, then gently spread the onion mixture over the base of the pastry shell. Whisk together the cream, eggs, blue cheese, thyme and freshly ground black pepper to taste. Pour into the pastry shell and bake for 35 minutes, or until firm.

Roll the pastry out thinly and line the greased flan tin, trimming away any excess.

Spread the onion mixture over the cooled pastry base, then pour in the cream mixture.

NUTRITION PER SERVE
Protein 9 g; Fat 30 g; Carbohydrate 25 g; Dietary Fibre 1.5 g; Cholesterol 145 mg; 1718 kJ (410 Cal)

Tofu pastries

PREPARATION TIME: 30 MINUTES + 4 HOURS REFRIGERATION | TOTAL COOKING TIME: 20 MINUTES | SERVES 4

150 g (5½ oz) firm tofu
2 spring onions (scallions), chopped
3 teaspoons chopped coriander (cilantro) leaves
½ teaspoon grated orange zest
2 teaspoons soy sauce
1 tablespoon sweet chilli sauce
2 teaspoons grated fresh ginger
1 teaspoon cornflour (cornstarch)
60 g (2¼ oz/¼ cup) sugar
125 ml (4 fl oz/½ cup) rice vinegar
1 small Lebanese (short) cucumber, finely diced
1 small red chilli, thinly sliced
1 spring onion (scallion), extra, thinly sliced on the diagonal
2 sheets ready-rolled puff pastry
1 egg, lightly beaten

1 Drain the tofu, then pat dry and cut into small cubes.

2 Put the spring onion, coriander, zest, soy and chilli sauces, ginger, cornflour and tofu in a bowl and mix. Cover. Refrigerate for 3–4 hours.

3 To make the dipping sauce, place the sugar and vinegar in a small saucepan and stir over low heat until the sugar dissolves. Remove from the heat and add the cucumber, chilli and extra spring onion. Cool completely.

4 Preheat the oven to 220°C (425°F/Gas 7). Cut each pastry sheet into four squares. Drain the filling and divide into eight. Place one portion in the centre of each square and brush the edges with egg. Fold into a triangle and seal the edges with a fork.

5 Put the triangles on two lined baking trays, brush with egg and bake for 15 minutes. Serve with the sauce.

NUTRITION PER SERVE
Protein 9 g; Fat 24 g; Carbohydrate 48 g; Dietary Fibre 2 g; Cholesterol 66 mg; 1946 kJ (464 Cal)

Gently mix the tofu and other ingredients together in a bowl.

Fold the pastry to enclose the filling, then seal the edges with a fork.

Spinach and feta triangles

PREPARATION TIME: 30 MINUTES | TOTAL COOKING TIME: 40 MINUTES | MAKES 8

1 kg (2 lb 4 oz) English spinach, roughly chopped
3 tablespoons olive oil
1 onion, chopped
10 spring onions (scallions), sliced
1 large handful chopped parsley
1 tablespoon chopped dill
large pinch of ground nutmeg
35 g (1¼ oz/⅓ cup) grated parmesan cheese
150 g (5½ oz) crumbled feta cheese
90 g (3¼ oz) ricotta cheese
4 eggs, lightly beaten
40 g (1½ oz) butter, melted
1 tablespoon olive oil, extra
12 sheets filo pastry

1 Wash the spinach leaves and place in a large saucepan with a little water on the leaves. Cover and cook over low heat for 5 minutes, or until the leaves have wilted. Drain and allow to cool slightly before squeezing tightly to remove any excess water.

2 Heat the oil in a heavy-based frying pan. Add the onion and cook over low heat for 10 minutes, or until golden. Add the spring onion and cook for a further 3 minutes. Remove from heat. Stir in the drained spinach, herbs, nutmeg, cheeses and egg. Season well.

3 Preheat the oven to180°C (350°F/Gas 4). Grease two baking trays. Combine the melted butter with the extra oil. Work with three sheets of pastry at a time, keeping the rest covered with a damp tea towel (dish towel). Brush each sheet with the butter mixture and lay on top of each other. Cut in half lengthways.

4 Spoon 4 tablespoons of the filling on an angle at the end of each strip. Fold the pastry over to enclose the filling and form a triangle. Continue folding over until you reach the end of the pastry. Put the triangles on baking trays and brush with the remaining butter mixture. Bake for 20–25 minutes, or until golden brown.

VARIATION: If spinach isn't in season you can use silverbeet instead. Use the same quantity and trim the coarse white stems from the leaves.

NUTRITION PER TRIANGLE
Protein 15 g; Fat 25 g; Carbohydrate 10 g; Dietary Fibre 4.5 g; Cholesterol 125 mg; 1325 kJ (315 Cal)

Brush each sheet of filo pastry with the mixture of butter and oil.

Spoon the filling onto the end of the pastry at an angle. Fold the pastry over it to make a triangle.

Continue folding the triangle parcel until you reach the end of the pastry sheet.

Cheese and chive tart

PREPARATION TIME: 40 MINUTES | TOTAL COOKING TIME: 55 MINUTES | SERVES 6–8

80 g (2¾ oz) butter
40 g (1½ oz/⅓ cup) plain (all-purpose) flour, sifted
250 ml (9 fl oz/1 cup) pouring (whipping) cream
170 ml (5½ fl oz/⅔ cup) sour cream
4 eggs, separated
125 g (4½ oz) gruyère cheese, grated
3 tablespoons snipped chives
¼ teaspoon ground nutmeg
pinch of cayenne pepper
6 sheets filo pastry

1 Preheat the oven to 190°C (375°F/Gas 5). Grease a deep loose-based fluted flan (tart) tin measuring 20 cm (8 inches) across the base. Melt half the butter in a saucepan. Add the flour and cook, stirring, for 1 minute. Remove from the heat and gradually whisk in the cream and sour cream.

2 Return to the heat and whisk constantly until the mixture boils and thickens. Remove from the heat and whisk in the egg yolks. Cover with plastic wrap and set aside to cool slightly. Whisk in the cheese, chives, nutmeg and cayenne pepper.

3 Melt the remaining butter and brush some over each sheet of pastry. Fold each one in half and use to line the tin, allowing the edges to overhang.

4 Beat the egg whites until stiff peaks form, then stir a spoonful into the cheese mixture to loosen it up a little. Gently fold in the rest. Spoon the mixture into the pastry shell and bake for 20–25 minutes, or until puffed and golden. Serve immediately.

NUTRITION PER SERVE (8)
Protein 10 g; Fat 40 g; Carbohydrate 15 g; Dietary Fibre 1 g; Cholesterol 200 mg; 1895 kJ (450 Cal)

Roasted pumpkin and spinach quiche

PREPARATION TIME: 20 MINUTES | TOTAL COOKING TIME: 1 HOUR 50 MINUTES | SERVES 4–6

500 g (1 lb 2 oz) butternut pumpkin (squash)
1 red onion, cut into small wedges
2 tablespoons olive oil
1 garlic clove, crushed
4 eggs
125 ml (4 fl oz/½ cup) pouring (whipping) cream
125 ml (4 fl oz/½ cup) milk
1 tablespoon chopped parsley
1 tablespoon chopped coriander (cilantro)
1 teaspoon wholegrain mustard
6 sheets filo pastry
50 g (1¾ oz) English spinach, blanched
1 tablespoon grated parmesan cheese

1 Preheat the oven to 190°C (375°F/Gas 5). Slice the pumpkin into 1 cm (½ inch) pieces, leaving the skin on. Place the pumpkin, onion, 1 tablespoon of the olive oil, garlic and 1 teaspoon of salt in a roasting tin. Roast for 1 hour, or until lightly golden and cooked.

2 Whisk together the eggs, cream, milk, herbs and mustard. Season with salt and freshly ground black pepper.

3 Grease a loose-based fluted flan (tart) tin or ovenproof dish measuring 22 cm (8½ inches) across the base. Brush each sheet of filo pastry with oil and then line the flan tin with the six sheets. Fold the sides down, tucking them into the tin to form a crust.

4 Heat a baking tray in the oven for 10 minutes. Place the flan tin on the tray and arrange all the vegetables over the base. Pour the egg mixture over the vegetables and sprinkle with the parmesan.

5 Bake for 35–40 minutes, or until the filling is golden brown and set.

NUTRITION PER SERVE (6)
Protein 10 g; Fat 20 g; Carbohydrate 15 g; Dietary Fibre 2 g; Cholesterol 155 mg; 1200 kJ (285 Cal)

Pour the mixture of egg and cream over the vegetables in the tin.

Fold the sides of the filo pastry down and tuck them into the tin to form a crust.

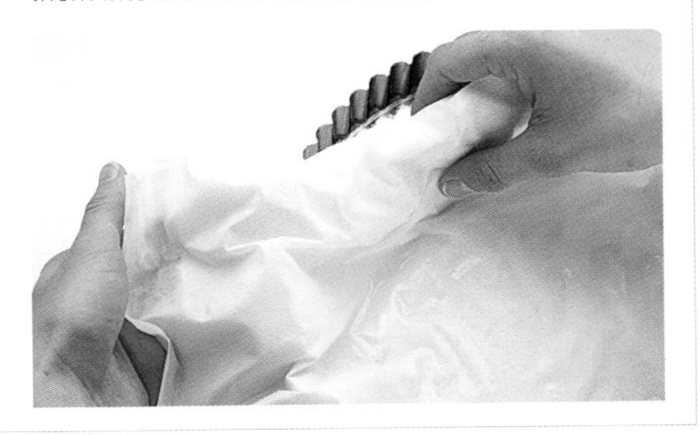

Roasted tomato and zucchini tartlets

PREPARATION TIME: 45 MINUTES | TOTAL COOKING TIME: 1 HOUR 20 MINUTES | SERVES 6

3 roma (plum) tomatoes, halved lengthways
1 teaspoon balsamic vinegar
1 teaspoon olive oil
3 small zucchini (courgettes), sliced
3 sheets ready-rolled puff pastry
1 egg yolk, beaten, to glaze
12 small black olives
24 capers, drained and rinsed

PISTACHIO MINT PESTO

75 g (2½ oz/½ cup) unsalted shelled pistachio nuts
2 large handfuls mint leaves
2 garlic cloves, crushed
4 tablespoons olive oil
50 g (1¾ oz/½ cup) grated parmesan cheese

NUTRITION PER SERVE
Protein 15 g; Fat 60 g; Carbohydrate 35 g; Dietary Fibre 6 g; Cholesterol 80 mg; 3040 kJ (725 Cal)

1 Preheat the oven to 150°C (300°F/Gas 2). Place the tomato, cut side up, on a baking tray. Roast for 30 minutes, then brush with the combined vinegar and oil a nd roast for a further 30 minutes. Increase the oven to 210°C (415°F/Gas 6–7).

2 To make the pesto, place the pistachios, mint and garlic in a processor and process for 15 seconds. With the motor running, slowly pour in the olive oil. Add the parmesan and process briefly.

3 Preheat the grill (broiler) and line with foil. Place the zucchini in a single layer on the foil and brush with the remaining balsamic vinegar and oil. Grill (broil) for about 5 minutes, turning once.

4 Roll the pastry out to 25 x 40 cm (10 x 16 inches) and cut out six 12 cm (4½ inch) circles. Put on a greased baking tray and brush with egg yolk. Spread a tablespoon of pesto on each, leaving a 2 cm (¾ inch) border. Divide the zucchini among the pastries and top with the tomato halves. Bake for 15 minutes, or until golden. Top with olives, capers and freshly ground black pepper.

Roast the tomatoes for 30 minutes, then brush with the vinegar and oil.

Add the grated parmesan to the pesto and process briefly until well mixed.

Arrange a few grilled zucchini slices over the pesto, leaving a clear border.

Pasta

Ricotta lasagne

PREPARATION TIME: 1 HOUR | TOTAL COOKING TIME: 1 HOUR 30 MINUTES | SERVES 8

500 g (1 lb 2 oz) fresh lasagne sheets
1 large handful basil leaves, coarsely chopped
2 tablespoons fresh breadcrumbs
3 tablespoons pine nuts
2 teaspoons paprika
1 tablespoon grated parmesan cheese

RICOTTA FILLING

750 g (1 lb 10 oz) ricotta cheese
50 g (1¾ oz/½ cup) grated parmesan
pinch of nutmeg

TOMATO SAUCE

1 tablespoon olive oil
2 onions, chopped
2 garlic cloves, crushed
800 g (1 lb 12 oz) tin chopped tomatoes
1 tablespoon tomato paste (concentrated purée)

BECHAMEL SAUCE

60 g (2¼ oz) butter
60 g (2¼ oz/½ cup) plain (all-purpose) flour
500 ml (17 fl oz/2 cups) milk
2 eggs, lightly beaten
35 g (1¼ oz/⅓ cup) grated parmesan cheese

NUTRITION PER SERVE
Protein 28 g; Fat 30 g; Carbohydrate 60 g; Dietary Fibre 4.5 g; Cholesterol 130 mg; 2622 kJ (625 Cal)

1 Lightly grease a 25 x 32 cm (10 x 13 inch) ovenproof dish.

2 To make ricotta filling, put the cheeses, nutmeg and pepper in a bowl and mix together.

3 To make the tomato sauce, heat the oil in a frying pan, add the onion. Cook for 10 minutes, stirring occasionally, until very soft. Add the garlic and cook for 1 minute. Add the tomato and tomato paste. Stir until the mixture boils, then reduce the heat and simmer uncovered for 15 minutes, or until thickened, stirring occasionally.

4 To make the béchamel sauce, heat the butter in a small saucepan. When starting to foam, add the flour and stir for 3 minutes, or until just coloured. Remove from the heat; add milk gradually, stirring after each addition; return to heat and stir until the sauce boils and thickens. Remove from heat and stir in the eggs. Return to moderate heat and stir until almost boiling. Add the cheese and season to taste. Cover the surface with plastic wrap to prevent a skin forming. Preheat the oven to 200°C (400°F/Gas 6).

5 Put a layer of lasagne sheets in the dish. Spread with a third of the filling, sprinkle with basil, then top with a third of the tomato sauce. Repeat the layers, finishing with pasta. Pour over the béchamel and smooth out. Sprinkle with combined breadcrumbs, pine nuts, paprika and parmesan. Bake for 45 minutes. Leave for 10 minutes before serving.

Heat the butter in a small pan. When starting to foam, add the flour and stir until just coloured.

Add the milk gradually, stirring after each addition, return to heat and stir until sauce boils and thickens.

Spread with a third of the ricotta, sprinkle with basil, then top with one-third of the tomato sauce.

Fettuccine with green olive and eggplant

PREPARATION TIME: 20 MINUTES | TOTAL COOKING TIME: 20 MINUTES | SERVES 4

500 g (1 lb 2 oz) fettuccine
185 g (6½ oz/1 cup) green olives
1 large eggplant (aubergine)
2 tablespoons olive oil
2 garlic cloves, crushed
125 ml (4 fl oz/½ cup) lemon juice
2 tablespoons chopped parsley
50 g (1¾ oz/½ cup) grated parmesan cheese

1 Cook the pasta in a large saucepan of rapidly boiling salted water until *al dente*. Drain well and return to the pan to keep warm. While the pasta is cooking, chop the olives (removing the pits) and cut the eggplant into small cubes.

2 Heat the oil in a heavy-based frying pan. Add the garlic and stir for 30 seconds. Add the eggplant and cook over medium heat, stirring frequently, for 6 minutes or until the eggplant is tender.

3 Add the olives, lemon juice, salt and freshly ground black pepper to the pan. Tip the sauce into the pasta and toss well. Serve sprinkled with parsley and parmesan.

HINT *Eggplant can sometimes be bitter. To draw out the bitter juices, put it in a colander, sprinkle with salt and leave for 30 minutes. Rinse well.*

While the pasta is cooking, dice the eggplant and chop the olives.

Add the olives, lemon juice and salt and pepper to the frying pan, then tip over the pasta.

NUTRITION PER SERVE
Protein 20 g; Fat 17 g; Carbohydrate 92 g; Dietary Fibre 10 g; Cholesterol 12 mg; 2572 kJ (615 Cal)

Pasta with ricotta, chilli and herbs

PREPARATION TIME: 15 MINUTES | TOTAL COOKING TIME: 20 MINUTES | SERVES 4

500 g (1 lb 2 oz) spiral pasta or penne
3 tablespoons olive oil
3 garlic cloves, crushed
2 teaspoons very finely chopped chilli
2 large handfuls flat-leaf (Italian) parsley leaves, roughly chopped
2 small handfuls basil leaves, shredded
1 large handful oregano leaves, roughly chopped
200 g (7 oz) ricotta cheese, cut into small cubes

1 Add the pasta to a large saucepan of rapidly boiling salted water and cook until *al dente*. Drain well and return to the pan to keep warm. Meanwhile, heat the oil in a non-stick heavy-based frying pan. Add the garlic and chilli and stir for 1 minute over low heat.

2 Pour the contents of the frying pan over the pasta and add the herbs. Season to taste and toss well.

3 Add the cubes of ricotta to the pasta and serve immediately.

NOTE: *Fresh ricotta cheese is sold in delicatessens. Use within 2 days.*

NUTRITION PER SERVE
Protein 20 g; Fat 20 g; Carbohydrate 90 g; Dietary Fibre 7 g; Cholesterol 24 mg; 2635 kJ (630 Cal)

Heat the oil in a frying pan and cook the garlic and chilli for 1 minute over low heat.

Pour the contents of the frying pan over the pasta and add the herbs and salt and pepper.

Cut the fresh ricotta into small cubes and add to the pasta.

Spinach and ricotta cannelloni

PREPARATION TIME: 45 MINUTES | TOTAL COOKING TIME: 1 HOUR | SERVES 4

375 g (13 oz) packet fresh lasagne
75 g (2½ oz/½ cup) grated mozzarella cheese
50 g (1¾ oz/½ cup) grated parmesan cheese

FILLING
30 g (1 oz) butter
1 small onion, finely chopped
2 garlic cloves, crushed
3 bunches English spinach, trimmed and finely shredded
300 g (10½ oz) ricotta cheese
1 tablespoon oregano

SAUCE
1 tablespoon olive oil
1 small onion, finely chopped
2 garlic cloves, crushed
440 g (15½ oz) tin peeled whole tomatoes
125 ml (4 fl oz/½ cup) tomato pasta sauce
1 teaspoon dried oregano
2 teaspoons dijon mustard
1 tablespoon balsamic vinegar
1 teaspoon sugar

NUTRITION PER SERVE
Protein 25 g; Fat 27 g; Carbohydrate 35 g; Dietary Fibre 5 g; Cholesterol 70 mg; 1970 kJ (470 Cal)

1 Preheat the oven to 180°C (350°F/Gas 4). Cut pasta sheets into twelve 12 cm (4½ inch) squares. Bring a saucepan of salted water to boil, blanch the lasagne in batches for 1–2 minutes, then drain flat on a damp tea towel (dish towel).

2 To make the filling, melt the butter in a pan and cook the onion and garlic for 3–5 minutes, or until onion softens. Add the spinach and cook for 5 minutes, or until wilted and the moisture has evaporated. Cool, then mix with the ricotta and oregano in a food processor until smooth. Season.

3 To make the sauce, heat the oil in a pan, add the onion and garlic and cook over low heat for 8–10 minutes. Add the rest of sauce ingredients. Bring to the boil, then reduce heat and simmer for 10–15 minutes, or until the sauce thickens.

4 Lightly grease a 2 litre (70 fl oz/8 cup) casserole dish. Spread one-third of the sauce over the base. Spoon 1½ tablespoons of the spinach mixture onto one side of each lasagne square, leaving a small border. Roll up pasta to cover filling and place in the dish seam side down. Repeat with all the sheets. Spoon in the remaining sauce and sprinkle with cheeses. Bake for 30–35 minutes, or until bubbling. Leave for 5 minutes before serving.

Blanch the lasagne sheets in batches in salted boiling water.

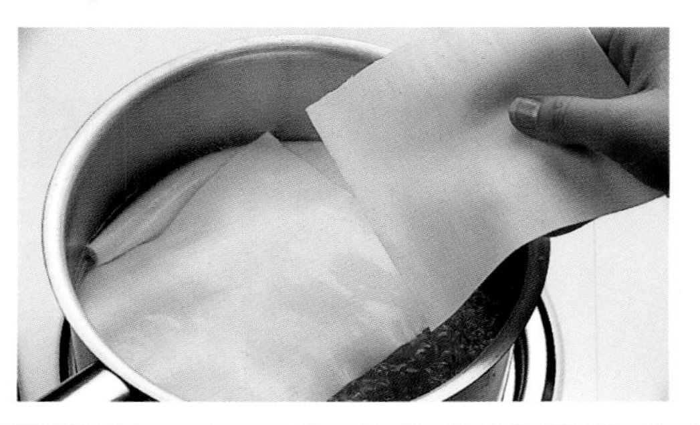

Lay the lasagne squares out flat on a clean damp tea towel to drain.

Spoon the spinach mixture onto one side of the pasta square and then roll up into a tube.

Macaroni cheese

PREPARATION TIME: 15 MINUTES | TOTAL COOKING TIME: 35 MINUTES | SERVES 4

225 g (8 oz) macaroni
80 g (2¾ oz) butter
1 onion, finely chopped
3 tablespoons plain (all-purpose) flour
500 ml (17 fl oz/2 cups) milk
2 teaspoons wholegrain mustard
250 g (9 oz) cheddar cheese, grated
30 g (1 oz) fresh breadcrumbs

1 Cook the pasta in rapidly boiling salted water until *al dente.* Drain. Preheat the oven to 180°C (350°F/Gas 4) and grease a casserole dish.

2 Melt the butter in a large saucepan over low heat and cook the onion for 5 minutes, or until softened. Stir in the flour and cook for 1 minute, or until pale and foaming. Remove from the heat and gradually stir in the milk. Return to the heat and stir until the sauce boils and thickens. Reduce the heat and simmer for 2 minutes. Stir in the mustard and about three-quarters of the cheese. Season to taste.

3 Mix the pasta with the cheese sauce. Spoon into the dish and sprinkle the breadcrumbs and remaining cheese over the top. Bake for 15 minutes, or until golden brown and bubbling.

NUTRITION PER SERVE
Protein 30 g; Fat 45 g; Carbohydrate 60 g; Dietary Fibre 4 g; Cholesterol 130 mg; 3087 kJ (737 Cal)

Cook the onion in the butter over low heat until softened.

Pumpkin rigatoni

PREPARATION TIME: 15 MINUTES | TOTAL COOKING TIME: 25 MINUTES | SERVES 4–6

3 tablespoons pine nuts
30 g (1 oz) butter
2 leeks, white part only, finely sliced
1 kg (2 lb 4 oz) pumpkin (winter squash), diced
½ teaspoon ground nutmeg
500 g (1 lb 2 oz) rigatoni or large penne
300 ml (10½ fl oz/1¼ cups) pouring (whipping) cream

1 Toast the pine nuts by stirring over low heat in a non-stick frying pan, until lightly golden. Alternatively, spread on a baking tray and grill (broil)—check often as they brown quickly.

2 Heat the butter in a large saucepan over low heat. Add the leek, cover and cook, stirring occasionally, for 5 minutes. Add the pumpkin and nutmeg, cover and cook for 8 minutes.

3 Meanwhile, cook the pasta in a large saucepan of rapidly boiling salted water until *al dente.* Drain and return to pan to keep warm.

4 Add the cream and 3 tablespoons water to the pumpkin and bring the sauce to the boil. Cook, stirring occasionally, for 8 minutes or until tender. Pour over the pasta. Sprinkle with the pine nuts to serve.

NUTRITION PER SERVE
Protein 15 g; Fat 30 g; Carbohydrate 72 g; Dietary Fibre 7 g; Cholesterol 80 mg; 2612 kJ (625 Cal)

Cut off the dark green leaves of the leek and slice the white part finely.

Heat the butter in a large saucepan and cook the sliced leek for 5 minutes.

Add the cream and a little water to the pumpkin and bring to the boil.

Sweet potato ravioli

PREPARATION TIME: 45 MINUTES | TOTAL COOKING TIME: 1 HOUR 10 MINUTES | SERVES 6

500 g (1 lb 2 oz) orange sweet potato, cut into large pieces
3 tablespoons olive oil
150 g (5½ oz) ricotta cheese
1 tablespoon chopped basil
1 garlic clove, crushed
2 tablespoons grated parmesan cheese
2 x 250 g (9 oz) packets egg won ton wrappers
60 g (2¼ oz) butter
4 spring onions (scallions), sliced on the diagonal
2 garlic cloves, extra, crushed
300 ml (10½ fl oz) pouring (whipping) cream
baby basil leaves, to serve

NUTRITION PER SERVE
Protein 11 g; Fat 40 g; Carbohydrate 35 g; Dietary Fibre 2.5 g; Cholesterol 105 mg; 2351 kJ (560 Cal)

1 Preheat the oven to 220°C (425°F/Gas 7). Place the sweet potato on a baking tray and drizzle with oil. Bake for 40 minutes, or until golden and tender.

2 Transfer the sweet potato to a bowl with the ricotta, basil, garlic and parmesan and mash until smooth.

3 Cover the won ton wrappers with a damp tea towel (dish towel). Place 2 level teaspoons of the sweet potato mixture into the centre of one wrapper and brush the edges with a little water. Top with another wrapper. Place onto a baking tray lined with baking paper and cover with a tea towel. Repeat with the remaining ingredients to make 60 ravioli, placing a sheet of baking paper between each layer.

4 Melt the butter in a frying pan. Add the spring onion and garlic and cook over medium heat for 1 minute. Add the cream, bring to the boil, then reduce the heat and simmer for 4–5 minutes, or until the cream has reduced and thickened. Keep warm.

5 Bring a large saucepan of water to the boil. Cook the ravioli in batches for 2–4 minutes, or until just tender. Drain well. Ladle the hot sauce over the top of the ravioli, garnish with the basil leaves and serve immediately.

Drizzle the chunks of sweet potato with oil and bake until golden.

Cover the filling with a won ton wrapper, lining it up with the bottom wrapper.

Cook the ravioli in batches so that the pan is not overcrowded. Cook until tender.

Warm pesto pasta salad

PREPARATION TIME: 20 MINUTES | TOTAL COOKING TIME: 20 MINUTES | SERVES 4

PESTO
2 garlic cloves, crushed
1 teaspoon sea salt
3 tablespoons pine nuts, toasted
2 very large handfuls basil
50 g (1¾ oz/½ cup) grated parmesan cheese
4 tablespoons extra virgin olive oil
500 g (1 lb 2 oz) orecchiette or shell pasta
2 tablespoons olive oil
150 g (5½ oz) jar capers, drained, rinsed and patted dry
2 tablespoons extra virgin olive oil
2 garlic cloves, chopped
3 tomatoes, seeded and diced
300 g (10½ oz) asparagus spears, blanched
2 tablespoons balsamic vinegar
200 g (7 oz) rocket (arugula)
parmesan shavings, to serve

1 To make the pesto, place garlic, sea salt and pine nuts in a food processor and process until combined. Add basil and parmesan and process until finely minced. With the motor running, add oil in thin steady stream and blend until smooth.

2 Cook the pasta in a large saucepan of boiling water until *al dente,* then drain well. Meanwhile, heat the oil in a frying pan, add capers and fry over high heat, stirring occasionally, for 4–5 minutes, or until crisp. Remove from pan and drain on crumpled paper towels. In the same frying pan, heat the extra virgin olive oil over medium heat and add the garlic, tomato and asparagus. Cook for 1–2 minutes, tossing well. Stir in the balsamic vinegar.

3 Drain the pasta and transfer to a large serving bowl. Add the pesto and toss, coating the pasta well. Cool slightly. Add the tomato mixture and rocket and season to taste with salt and freshly ground black pepper. Toss well and sprinkle with the capers and parmesan. Serve warm.

Fry the capers over high heat, stirring occasionally, until crisp.

Add the pesto and toss thoroughly through the pasta. Allow to cool a little.

NUTRITION PER SERVE
Protein 22 g; Fat 45 g; Carbohydrate 90 g; Dietary Fibre 9 g; Cholesterol 12 mg; 3629 kJ (868 Cal)

Pasta napolitana

PREPARATION TIME: 20 MINUTES | TOTAL COOKING TIME: 1 HOUR | SERVES 4–6

2 tablespoons olive oil
1 onion, finely chopped
1 carrot, finely chopped
1 celery stalk, finely chopped
500 g (1 lb 2 oz) very ripe tomatoes, chopped
2 tablespoons chopped parsley
2 teaspoons sugar
500 g (1 lb 2 oz) pasta (see NOTE)

1 Heat the oil in a heavy-based saucepan. Add the onion, carrot and celery, cover and cook for 10 minutes over low heat, stirring occasionally.

2 Add the tomato, parsley, sugar and 125 ml (4 fl oz/½ cup) water. Bring to the boil, reduce the heat to low, cover and simmer for 45 minutes, stirring occasionally. Season. If necessary, add up to 185 ml (6 fl oz/¾ cup) more water.

3 About 15 minutes before serving, cook the pasta in a large pan of rapidly boiling salted water until *al dente*. Drain well and return to the pan to keep warm. Pour the sauce over the pasta and gently toss.

NOTE: *Traditionally, spaghetti is served with this sauce, but you can use any pasta.*

HINT: *The sauce can be reduced to a more concentrated version by cooking it uncovered so the moisture evaporates, for a longer period. Store it in the refrigerator and add water or stock to thin it, if necessary, when you are reheating.*

Dice the vegetables quite finely before cooking in the hot oil.

The tomatoes should be very ripe to give this sauce the best flavour.

NUTRITION PER SERVE (6):
Protein 10 g; Fat 7 g; Carbohydrate 65 g; Dietary Fibre 6 g; Cholesterol 0 mg; 1540 kJ (365 Cal)

Herb ravioli

PREPARATION TIME: 1 HOUR + 30 MINUTES STANDING | TOTAL COOKING TIME: 10 MINUTES | SERVES 4

300 g (10½ oz) plain (all-purpose) flour
3 eggs, beaten
3 tablespoons oil
250 g (9 oz/1 cup) ricotta cheese
2 tablespoons grated parmesan cheese
2 teaspoons snipped chives
1 tablespoon chopped flat-leaf (Italian) parsley
2 teaspoons chopped basil
1 teaspoon chopped lemon thyme or thyme
1 egg, extra, beaten

NUTRITION PER SERVE
Protein 25 g; Fat 30 g; Carbohydrate 55 g; Dietary Fibre 3 g; Cholesterol 215 mg; 2395 kJ (570 Cal)

1 Sift flour into a bowl and make a well in the centre. Gradually mix in the eggs and oil. Turn out onto a lightly floured surface and knead for 6 minutes, or until smooth. Cover with plastic wrap and leave for 30 minutes.

2 To make the filling, mix the ricotta, parmesan and herbs. Season well.

3 Divide the dough into four portions and shape each into a log. Keeping unworked portions covered, take one portion and flatten it with a rolling pin. Roll each portion out as thinly as possible into rectangles, making 2 slightly larger and wider than the others.

4 Spread one of the smaller sheets out onto a work surface. Spoon 1 teaspoon of the filling at 5 cm (2 inch) intervals. Brush the beaten egg between the filling along the cutting lines. Place a larger sheet on top. Press the two sheets together along the cutting line. Cut the ravioli with a pastry wheel or knife. Transfer to a lightly floured baking tray. Repeat with the remaining sheets and filling. Can be stored in the refrigerator for 1–2 days.

5 Cook the ravioli in a large pan of salted boiling water for 5–8 minutes and top with a sauce of your choice.

Mix together the ricotta, parmesan and herbs and season with salt and pepper.

Brush the beaten egg between the filling along the cutting lines.

Press the two sheets of dough together and cut the ravioli with a pastry wheel.

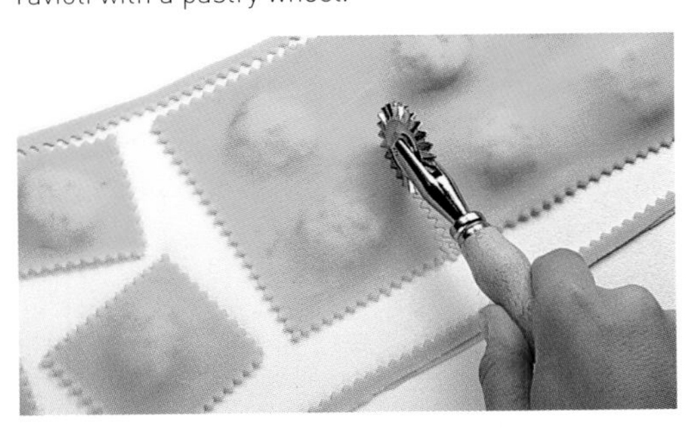

Pasta alfredo

PREPARATION TIME: 10 MINUTES | TOTAL COOKING TIME: 15 MINUTES | SERVES 4–6

500 g (1 lb 2 oz) pasta (see NOTE)
90 g (3¼ oz) butter
150 g (5½ oz/1½ cups) grated parmesan cheese
315 ml (10¾ fl oz/1¼ cups) pouring (whipping) cream
3 tablespoons chopped parsley

1 Cook the pasta in a large pan of rapidly boiling salted water until *al dente*. Drain well and return to the pan to keep warm.

2 While the pasta is cooking, melt the butter in a saucepan over low heat. Add the parmesan and cream and bring to the boil, stirring constantly. Reduce the heat and simmer, stirring, until the sauce has thickened slightly. Add the parsley, season to taste, and stir until well combined.

3 Add the sauce to the pasta and toss well so the sauce coats the pasta. Garnish with chopped herbs or sprigs of fresh herbs such as thyme.

NOTE: *Traditionally fettucine is used with this sauce, but you can try any pasta. Try to time the sauce so it is ready just as the pasta is cooked.*

It is best to use a block of parmesan and grate your own each time you need it.

To chop parsley, use a large sharp knife. A swivel action is easiest, holding the point of the knife.

NUTRITION PER SERVE (6):
Protein 20 g; Fat 40 g; Carbohydrate 60 g; Dietary Fibre 4 g; Cholesterol 125 mg; 2875 kJ (685 Cal)

Fettuccine with zucchini

PREPARATION TIME: 15 MINUTES | TOTAL COOKING TIME: 15 MINUTES | SERVES 4–6

500 g (1 lb 2 oz) fettuccine or tagliatelle
60 g (2¼ oz) butter
2 garlic cloves, crushed
500 g (1 lb 2 oz) zucchini (courgettes), grated
75 g (2½ oz/¾ cup) grated parmesan cheese
250 ml (9 fl oz/1 cup) olive oil
16 basil leaves (see HINT)

1 Cook the pasta in a large saucepan of rapidly boiling salted water until *al dente.* Drain well and return to the pan to keep warm.

2 Meanwhile, heat the butter in a deep heavy-based saucepan over low heat until it is foaming. Add the garlic and cook for 1 minute. Add the zucchini and cook, stirring occasionally, for 1–2 minutes or until the zucchini has softened.

3 Add the sauce to the pasta. Add the parmesan and toss well.

4 To make basil leaves crisp, heat the oil in a small saucepan, add two leaves at a time and cook for 1 minute or until crisp. Drain on paper towels. Serve with the pasta.

HINT: *Basil leaves can be fried up to 2 hours in advance of preparing this dish. Store in an airtight container after cooling.*

NUTRITION PER SERVE (6)
Protein 15 g; Fat 53 g; Carbohydrate 60 g; Dietary Fibre 5.5 g; Cholesterol 37 mg; 3245 kJ (775 Cal)

Coarsely grate the zucchini and then fry with the garlic until softened.

Toss the zucchini into the pasta and then add the grated parmesan.

Fry the basil leaves in a little oil until they are crisp, then drain on paper towels.

Pumpkin and basil lasagne

PREPARATION TIME: 20 MINUTES | TOTAL COOKING TIME: 1 HOUR 25 MINUTES | SERVES 4

650 g (1 lb 7 oz) pumpkin (winter squash)
2 tablespoons olive oil
500 g (1 lb 2 oz) ricotta cheese
50 g (1¾ oz/⅓ cup) pine nuts, toasted
1 large handful basil
2 garlic cloves, crushed
35 g (1¼ oz) parmesan cheese, grated
125 g (4½ oz) fresh lasagne sheets
185 g (6½ oz) mozzarella cheese, grated

NUTRITION PER SERVE
Protein 24 g; Fat 32 g; Carbohydrate 33 g; Dietary Fibre 4.5 g; Cholesterol 37 mg; 2166 kJ (517 Cal)

1 Preheat the oven to 180°C (350°F/Gas 4). Lightly grease a baking tray. Cut the pumpkin into thin slices and arrange in a single layer on the tray. Brush with oil and cook for 1 hour, or until softened, turning the slices halfway through cooking.

2 Place the ricotta, pine nuts, basil, garlic and parmesan in a bowl and mix well with a wooden spoon.

3 Brush a square 20 cm (8 inch) ovenproof dish with oil. Cook the pasta according to the packet instructions. Arrange one-third of the pasta sheets over the base of the dish and spread with the ricotta mixture. Top with half of the remaining lasagne sheets.

4 Arrange the pumpkin evenly over the pasta with as few gaps as possible. Season with salt and freshly ground black pepper and top with the final layer of pasta sheets. Sprinkle with mozzarella. Bake for 20–25 minutes, or until the cheese is golden. Leave for 10 minutes, then cut into squares.

NOTE: *If the pasta has no cooking instructions, blanch them one at a time until softened. Then drain and spread on tea towels (dish towels) to dry.*

Mix together the ricotta, pine nuts, basil, garlic and parmesan.

Cook the pasta according to the packet instructions until *al dente*.

Place the pumpkin on top of the lasagne sheet, leaving as few gaps as possible.

Salads

Mexicana salad

PREPARATION TIME: 40 MINUTES + OVERNIGHT STANDING | TOTAL COOKING TIME: 1 HOUR | SERVES 10–12

250 g (9 oz) black-eyed peas
250 g (9 oz) red kidney beans
500 g (1 lb 2 oz) sweet potato
1 large red onion, chopped
1 large green capsicum (pepper), chopped
3 ripe tomatoes, chopped
2 small handfuls chopped basil
3 flour tortillas
1 tablespoon oil
2 tablespoons grated parmesan cheese
60 g (2¼ oz/¼ cup) sour cream

DRESSING
1 garlic clove, crushed
1 tablespoon lime juice
2 tablespoons olive oil

GUACAMOLE
3 ripe avocados
2 tablespoons lemon juice
1 garlic clove, crushed
1 small red onion, chopped
1 small red chilli, chopped
60 g (2¼ oz/¼ cup) sour cream
2 tablespoons hot ready-made taco sauce

1 Soak the peas and beans in a large bowl of cold water overnight. Drain and cook in a large saucepan of rapidly boiling water for 30 minutes, or until just tender. Skim off any scum that appears on the surface during cooking. Do not overcook or they will become mushy. Drain and set aside to cool.

2 Chop the sweet potato into large pieces and cook in boiling water until tender. Drain and combine with the onion, capsicum, tomato, peas and beans. Stir in the basil.

3 To make the dressing, shake the ingredients in a screw-top jar until combined. Pour over the salad and toss to coat.

4 Preheat the oven to 180°C (350°F/Gas 4). Using a small knife, cut large triangles out of the tortillas, brush each one lightly with the oil and sprinkle with parmesan. Bake for 5–10 minutes, or until they are crisp and golden.

5 To make the guacamole, mash the avocados with the lemon juice. Add the garlic, onion, chilli, sour cream and taco sauce and mix well.

6 Pile the guacamole in the centre of the salad, top with the sour cream and arrange the triangle chips on top.

Combine the sweet potato with the onion, capsicum, tomato and beans.

NUTRITION PER SERVE (12)
Protein 15 g; Fat 25 g; Carbohydrate 40 g; Dietary Fibre 10 g; Cholesterol 15 mg; 1735 kJ (415 Cal)

Asparagus and red capsicum salad

PREPARATION TIME: 20 MINUTES | TOTAL COOKING TIME: 15 MINUTES | SERVES 4

2 red capsicums (peppers)
4 tablespoons virgin olive oil
1 garlic clove, crushed
2 tablespoons lemon juice
2 tablespoons chopped basil
2 tablespoons pine nuts
310 g (11 oz) fresh asparagus
small black olives

1 Cut the capsicums into large pieces, removing the seeds and white membrane. Place, skin side up, under a hot grill (broiler) until the skin blackens and blisters. Cool under a tea towel (dish towel) or in a plastic bag, then carefully peel away and discard the skin. Finely dice the capsicum flesh.

2 Put the olive oil, garlic, lemon juice and basil in a small bowl and whisk to combine. Add the capsicum and pine nuts, and season with salt and freshly ground black pepper.

3 Remove the woody ends from the asparagus (hold each spear at both ends and bend gently—the woody end will snap off at its natural breaking point). Plunge the asparagus into a large frying pan of boiling water and cook for 3 minutes, or until just tender. Drain and plunge into a bowl of iced water, then drain again and gently pat dry with paper towels.

4 Arrange the asparagus on a large serving platter and spoon the dressing over the top. Garnish with the black olives and perhaps a few lemon wedges to squeeze over the top.

Grill the capsicum pieces until the skin blackens and blisters.

Cook the asparagus in boiling water, then plunge into cold water and pat dry with paper towels.

NUTRITION PER SERVE
Protein 4 g; Fat 25 g; Carbohydrate 5 g; Dietary Fibre 3 g; Cholesterol 0 mg; 1100 kJ (260 Cal)

Fresh beetroot and goat's cheese salad

PREPARATION TIME: 20 MINUTES | TOTAL COOKING TIME: 30 MINUTES | SERVES 4

1 kg (2 lb 4 oz) fresh beetroot (beets) (about 4 bulbs with leaves)
200 g (7 oz) green beans
1 tablespoon red wine vinegar
2 tablespoons extra virgin olive oil
1 garlic clove, crushed
1 tablespoon capers, drained, rinsed and coarsely chopped
100 g (3½ oz) goat's cheese

1 Trim the leaves from the beetroot. Scrub the bulbs and wash the leaves well. Simmer the whole bulbs in a large saucepan of boiling water, covered, for 30 minutes, or until tender when pierced with the point of a knife. (The cooking time may vary depending on the size of the bulbs.)

2 Meanwhile, bring a saucepan of water to the boil, add the beans and cook for 3 minutes, or until just tender. Remove with a slotted spoon and plunge into a bowl of cold water. Drain well. Add the beetroot leaves to the same saucepan of boiling water and cook for 3–5 minutes, or until the leaves and stems are tender. Drain, plunge into a bowl of cold water, then drain again well.

3 Drain and cool the beetroots, then peel the skins off and cut the bulbs into thin wedges.

4 To make the dressing, put the red wine vinegar, oil, garlic, capers, ½ teaspoon salt and ½ teaspoon freshly ground black pepper in a screw-top jar and shake.

5 To serve, divide the beans and beetroot (leaves and bulbs) among four serving plates. Crumble the goat's cheese over the top and drizzle with the dressing.

NUTRITION PER SERVE
Protein 12 g; Fat 18 g; Carbohydrate 22 g; Dietary Fibre 9 g; Cholesterol 25 mg; 1256 kJ (300 Cal)

Remove the skin from the beetroot, then cut into thin wedges.

Cook the beetroot leaves for 3–5 minutes, or until they are tender.

Caponata

PREPARATION TIME: 20 MINUTES + 24 HOURS REFRIGERATION | TOTAL COOKING TIME: 40 MINUTES | SERVES 8

1 kg (2 lb 4 oz) eggplant (aubergine), cubed
185 ml (6 fl oz/¾ cup) olive oil
200 g (7 oz) zucchini (courgettes), cubed
1 red capsicum (pepper), thinly sliced
2 onions, finely sliced
4 celery stalks, sliced
400 g (13 oz) tin chopped tomatoes
3 tablespoons red wine vinegar
2 tablespoons sugar
2 tablespoons drained and rinsed capers
24 green olives, pitted (see NOTE)
2 tablespoons pine nuts, toasted

NUTRITION PER SERVE
Protein 3.5 g; Fat 25 g; Carbohydrate 8.5 g; Dietary Fibre 5.5 g; Cholesterol 0 mg; 1160 kJ (280 Cal)

1 Put the eggplant in a colander, sprinkle with salt and leave to drain.

2 Heat 3 tablespoons of the oil in a large frying pan and fry the zucchini and capsicum for 5–6 minutes, or until the zucchini is lightly browned. Transfer to a bowl. Add a little more oil to the pan and gently fry the onion and celery for 6–8 minutes, or until softened but not brown. Transfer to the bowl.

3 Rinse the eggplant and pat dry. Add 3 tablespoons of the oil to the pan, increase the heat and brown the eggplant in batches. Keep adding more oil to each batch. Drain on paper towels and set aside.

4 Remove any excess oil from the frying pan and return the vegetables to the pan, except the eggplant.

5 Add 3 tablespoons water and the tomatoes. Reduce the heat, simmer for 10 minutes. Add the remaining ingredients and eggplant and mix well. Remove from the heat and cool. Cover and leave for 24 hours in the refrigerator. Add some pepper, and more vinegar if needed.

NOTE: *Green olives stuffed with red pimentos can be used instead of pitted green olives.*

STORAGE TIME: *Caponata will keep, covered, in the refrigerator for up to 5 days.*

You can remove the stones from the olives with an olive pitter.

Increase the heat under the oil and brown the eggplant in batches.

Add the water and chopped tomatoes to the frying pan and allow to simmer.

Leek and caper salad

PREPARATION TIME: 20 MINUTES | TOTAL COOKING TIME: 20 MINUTES | SERVES 6

5 leeks, white part only
4 tablespoons olive oil
2 tablespoons sherry vinegar
2 tablespoons baby capers, drained and rinsed

1 Cut the leeks in half lengthways and wash under cold running water. Cut them into 5 cm (2 inch) lengths, then cut in half again lengthways. Heat the oil in a large heavy-based frying pan, add the leeks and stir until coated with the oil. Cover and cook over low heat for 15–20 minutes, or until the leeks are soft and tender (but don't let them brown or burn). Cool for 10 minutes.

2 Stir through the vinegar and season to taste with salt and freshly ground black pepper. Transfer to a serving dish and scatter with the baby capers (if baby capers are unavailable, use chopped ordinary-sized capers).

NUTRITION PER SERVE
Protein 1.5 g; Fat 13 g; Carbohydrate 2.5 g; Dietary Fibre 2 g; Cholesterol 0 mg; 550 kJ (130 Cal)

Trim the leeks and wash them thoroughly under cold running water.

Add the leeks to the frying pan and stir until they are covered with the oil.

Add the vinegar to the cooled leeks and stir until they are well coated.

Potato salad

PREPARATION TIME: 15 MINUTES | TOTAL COOKING TIME: 5 MINUTES | SERVES 4

600 g (1 lb 5 oz) potatoes, unpeeled, cut into bite-sized pieces
1 small onion, finely chopped
1 small green capsicum (pepper), chopped
2–3 celery stalks, finely chopped
1 large handful parsley, finely chopped

DRESSING
185 g (6½ oz/¾ cup) mayonnaise
1–2 tablespoons vinegar or lemon juice
2 tablespoons sour cream

1 Cook the potato in a large pan of boiling water for 5 minutes, or until just tender (pierce with a sharp knife—if the potato yields easily it is ready). Drain and cool completely.

2 Combine the onion, capsicum, celery and parsley (reserving a little for garnishing) with the cooled potato in a large salad bowl.

3 To make the dressing, mix together the mayonnaise, vinegar and sour cream. Season with salt and freshly ground black pepper. Pour over the salad and toss gently to combine, without breaking the potato. Garnish with the remaining parsley.

NUTRITION PER SERVE
Protein 6 g; Fat 20 g; Carbohydrate 30 g; Dietary Fibre 4 g; Cholesterol 30 mg; 1355 kJ (320 Cal)

Cut the potatoes into bite-sized pieces, leaving the skins on.

Combine the onion, capsicum, celery and parsley with the cooled potato.

Mix together the mayonnaise, vinegar and sour cream and season, to taste.

Gado gado

PREPARATION TIME: 30 MINUTES | TOTAL COOKING TIME: 35 MINUTES | SERVES 4

6 new potatoes, unpeeled
2 carrots, cut into thick strips
250 g (9 oz) snake (yard-long) beans, cut into 10 cm (4 inch) lengths
2 tablespoons peanut oil
250 g (9 oz) firm tofu, cubed
100 g (3½ oz) baby English spinach
2 Lebanese (short) cucumbers, cut into thick strips
1 large red capsicum (pepper), cut into thick strips
100 g (3½ oz) bean sprouts
4 hard-boiled eggs

PEANUT SAUCE
1 tablespoon peanut oil
1 onion, finely chopped
160 g (5½ oz/⅔ cup) peanut butter
3 tablespoons kecap manis (see NOTE, page 42)
2 tablespoons ground coriander
2 teaspoons chilli sauce
185 ml (6 fl oz/¾cup) coconut cream
1 teaspoon grated palm sugar (jaggery)
1 tablespoon lemon juice

1 Cook the potatoes in boiling water until tender. Drain and cool slightly. Cut into quarters. Cook the carrots and beans separately in saucepans of boiling water until just tender. Plunge into iced water, then drain.

2 Heat the peanut oil in a non-stick frying pan and cook the tofu in batches until crisp. Drain on paper towels.

3 To make the peanut sauce, heat the peanut oil in a saucepan over low heat and cook the onion for 5 minutes, or until golden. Add the peanut butter, kecap manis (or sweetened soy sauce), coriander, chilli sauce and coconut cream. Bring to the boil, reduce the heat and simmer for 5 minutes. Add the palm sugar and juice and stir until dissolved.

4 Arrange all of the vegetables and tofu on a plate. Quarter the eggs and place in the centre. Serve with the sauce.

NUTRITION PER SERVE
Protein 35 g; Fat 55 g; Carbohydrate 35 g; Dietary Fibre 15 g; Cholesterol 265 mg; 3175 kJ (755 Cal)

Cut the cucumbers and capsicum into thick strips for dipping in the sauce.

Heat the oil and cook the tofu in batches until crisp and golden brown.

Add the peanut butter, kecap manis, coriander, chilli sauce and coconut cream.

Waldorf salad

PREPARATION TIME: 20 MINUTES | TOTAL COOKING TIME: NIL | SERVES 4–6

2 red apples
2 green apples
2 tablespoons lemon juice
30 g (1 oz/¼ cup) walnut pieces
4 celery stalks, sliced
250 g (9 oz/1 cup) mayonnaise
butter lettuce leaves, to serve

1 Quarter the apples, carefully remove and discard the seeds and cores, and cut the apples into small pieces.

2 Place the diced apple in a large bowl, drizzle with the lemon juice and toss to coat (this will prevent the apple discolouring). Add the walnut pieces and celery and mix well.

3 Add the mayonnaise to the apple mixture and toss until well coated. Spoon the salad into a lettuce-lined bowl and serve immediately.

NOTE: *Waldorf salad can be made up to 2 hours in advance and stored, covered, in the refrigerator. It is named after the Waldorf-Astoria hotel in New York where it was first served.*

NUTRITION PER SERVE (6)
Protein 2 g; Fat 15 g; Carbohydrate 20 g; Dietary Fibre 3 g; Cholesterol 15 mg; 1020 kJ (240 Cal)

Using both red and green apples gives the finished salad a colourful appearance.

Pour the lemon juice over the apples and toss to coat—this will prevent them browning.

Add the mayonnaise to the apple mixture and toss until well coated.

Stuffed mushroom salad

PREPARATION TIME: 25 MINUTES | TOTAL COOKING TIME: NIL | SERVES 4

20 button mushrooms
60 g (2¼ oz/¼ cup) pesto, chilled
100 g (3½ oz) rocket (arugula) leaves
1 green oakleaf lettuce
12 small black olives
50 g (1¾ oz/⅓ cup) sliced semi-dried (sun-blushed) or sun-dried tomatoes
1 tablespoon roughly chopped basil
parmesan cheese shavings, to serve

DRESSING
4 tablespoons olive oil
1 tablespoon white wine vinegar
1 teaspoon dijon mustard

1 Trim the mushroom stalks level with the caps and scoop out the remaining stalk with a melon baller. Spoon the pesto into the mushrooms.

2 To make the dressing, whisk together all the ingredients. Season with salt and freshly ground black pepper, to taste.

3 Arrange the rocket and lettuce leaves on a serving plate and top with the mushrooms, olives, tomato and basil. Drizzle the dressing over the salad and top with the parmesan shavings. Serve immediately.

HINT: *Home-made pesto is preferable for this recipe. To make your own, process 2 large handfuls basil leaves, 2 tablespoons pine nuts and 25 g (¾ oz/¼ cup) grated parmesan in a food processor to form a smooth paste. Gradually pour in 3 tablespoons olive oil in a steady stream with the motor running. Process until combined.*

Draw a vegetable peeler across a block of parmesan to make the shavings.

Spoon the chilled pesto into the mushroom caps. Home-made pesto will give the best flavour.

NUTRITION PER SERVE
Protein 9 g; Fat 35 g; Carbohydrate 2 g; Dietary Fibre 3 g; Cholesterol 15 mg; 1525 kJ (365 Cal)

Spicy lentil salad

PREPARATION TIME: 30 MINUTES | TOTAL COOKING TIME: 1 HOUR 10 MINUTES | SERVES 6

220 g (7¾ oz/1 cup) brown rice
185 g (6½ oz/1 cup) brown lentils
1 teaspoon turmeric
1 teaspoon ground cinnamon
6 cardamom pods
3 star anise
2 bay leaves
3 tablespoons sunflower oil
1 tablespoon lemon juice
250 g (9 oz) broccoli florets
2 carrots, cut into thin matchsticks
1 onion, finely chopped
2 garlic cloves, crushed
1 red capsicum (pepper), finely chopped
1 teaspoon garam masala
1 teaspoon ground coriander
250 g (9 oz/1½ cups) fresh or frozen peas, thawed

MINT AND YOGHURT DRESSING

250 g (9 oz/1 cup) plain yoghurt
1 tablespoon lemon juice
1 tablespoon chopped mint
1 teaspoon cumin seeds

1 Put 750 ml (26 fl oz/3 cups) water with the rice, lentils, turmeric, cinnamon, cardamom, star anise and bay leaves in a saucepan. Stir well and bring to the boil. Reduce the heat, cover and simmer gently for 50–60 minutes, or until the liquid is absorbed. Remove the whole spices. Transfer the mixture to a large bowl. Whisk 2 tablespoons of the sunflower oil with the lemon juice and fork through the rice mixture.

2 Boil, steam or microwave the broccoli and carrots until tender. Drain well and refresh in cold water.

3 Heat the remaining oil in a large saucepan and add the onion, garlic and capsicum. Stir-fry for 2–3 minutes, then add the garam masala and coriander, and stir-fry for a further 1–2 minutes. Add all of the vegetables and toss to coat in the spice mixture. Add to the rice and fork through to combine. Cover and refrigerate until cold.

4 To make the dressing, mix the yoghurt, lemon juice, mint and cumin seeds together, and season with salt and freshly ground black pepper. Spoon the salad into individual serving bowls or onto a platter and serve with the dressing.

NUTRITION PER SERVE
Protein 20 g; Fat 15 g; Carbohydrate 50 g; Dietary Fibre 10 g; Cholesterol 7 mg; 1605 kJ (380 Cal)

Add the cardamom pods, star anise and bay leaves to the pan.

Add all of the vegetables and toss to coat with the spice mixture.

Mix the yoghurt, lemon juice, mint and cumin seeds together to make the dressing.

Chickpea and roast vegetable salad

PREPARATION TIME: 25 MINUTES + 30 MINUTES STANDING | TOTAL COOKING TIME: 40 MINUTES | SERVES 8

500 g (1 lb 2 oz) butternut pumpkin (squash), cubed
2 red capsicums (peppers), halved
4 slender eggplants (aubergine), cut in half lengthways
4 zucchini (courgettes), cut in half lengthways
4 onions, quartered
olive oil, for brushing
2 x 400 g (14 oz) tins chickpeas, drained and rinsed
2 tablespoons chopped flat-leaf (Italian) parsley

DRESSING
4 tablespoons olive oil
2 tablespoons lemon juice
1 garlic clove, crushed
1 tablespoon chopped thyme

1 Preheat the oven to 220°C (425°F/Gas 7). Brush two baking trays with oil and lay out the vegetables in a single layer. Brush the vegetables lightly with oil.

2 Bake for 40 minutes, or until the vegetables are tender and begin to brown slightly on the edges. Cool. Remove the skins from the capsicum if you want. Chop the capsicum, eggplant and zucchini into pieces, then put the vegetables in a bowl with the chickpeas and half the parsley.

3 To make the dressing, whisk together all the dressing ingredients in a small bowl. Season, then toss with the vegetables. Leave for 30 minutes, then sprinkle with the rest of the parsley.

Rinse the chickpeas thoroughly under cold running water then drain.

Chop the roasted capsicum, eggplant and zucchini into small pieces.

NUTRITION PER SERVE
Protein 8.5 g; Fat 12 g; Carbohydrate 20 g; Dietary Fibre 7.5 g; Cholesterol 0 mg; 935 kJ (225 Cal)

Fennel with pecorino cheese

PREPARATION TIME: 15 MINUTES | TOTAL COOKING TIME: 25 MINUTES | SERVES 4

4 fennel bulbs
1 garlic clove, crushed
½ lemon, sliced
2 tablespoons olive oil
3 tablespoons butter, melted
2 tablespoons grated pecorino cheese

1 Cut the top shoots and base off the fennel and remove the tough outer layers. Cut into segments and place in a saucepan with the garlic, lemon, oil and 1 teaspoon of salt. Cover with water and bring to the boil. Reduce the heat and simmer for 20 minutes, or until just tender.

2 Drain well and place in a flameproof dish. Drizzle with the butter. Sprinkle with the cheese and season to taste.

3 Place under a preheated grill (broiler) until the cheese has browned. Best served piping hot.

NOTE: *If pecorino (a hard sheep's milk cheese) is not available, then use parmesan cheese instead.*

NUTRITION PER SERVE
Protein 4 g; Fat 23 g; Carbohydrate 3 g; Dietary Fibre 2.5 g; Cholesterol 43 mg; 990 kJ (235 Cal)

Trim the tops and bases from the fennel and remove the tough outer layers.

Cut the fennel into segments and put in a saucepan with the garlic, lemon, oil and salt.

Sprinkle grated pecorino cheese over the fennel and brown under a grill.

Warm radicchio salad with crushed tomato vinaigrette

PREPARATION TIME: 40 MINUTES | TOTAL COOKING TIME: 25 MINUTES | SERVES 4

4–5 tablespoons olive oil
6 garlic cloves, thinly sliced
7 roma (plum) tomatoes, cored and halved
3 tablespoons extra virgin olive oil
2 tablespoons red wine vinegar
1 teaspoon honey
900 g (2 lb) witlof (chicory/Belgian endive)
1 onion, halved and sliced
1 radicchio lettuce

NUTRITION PER SERVE
Protein 7 g; Fat 35 g; Carbohydrate 9 g; Dietary Fibre 8 g; Cholesterol 0 mg; 1620 kJ (385 Cal)

1 Heat half the olive oil in a small frying pan, add the garlic and fry over moderately high heat for a few minutes, or until lightly browned. Drain on paper towels.

2 Heat a little more olive oil in the frying pan and cook the tomatoes, cut side down, over moderate heat until browned and very soft. Turn to brown the other side. Transfer to a bowl to cool, then peel and discard the skins. Coarsely mash the flesh with a fork.

3 To make the vinaigrette, whisk together about half of the crushed tomatoes, the extra virgin olive oil, vinegar and honey. Season with salt and freshly ground black pepper.

4 Trim the coarse stems from the witlof, wash the leaves very well and drain. Cut into short lengths. Heat the rest of the olive oil in the frying pan, add the onion and cook until transparent. Add the witlof and stir until just wilted. Add the remaining tomatoes and stir until well combined. Season with salt and freshly ground black pepper.

5 Tear any large radicchio leaves into smaller pieces. Toss through the chicory mixture. Transfer to a large serving bowl, drizzle with the tomato vinaigrette and sprinkle with the garlic. Serve immediately.

Fry the garlic in the oil over moderate heat until lightly browned.

Cook the tomatoes until they are browned and very soft.

Tear any large radicchio leaves into smaller pieces and toss with the witlof.

Vietnamese salad

PREPARATION TIME: 30 MINUTES + 10 MINUTES STANDING + 30 MINUTES REFRIGERATION | TOTAL COOKING TIME: NIL | SERVES 4–6

200 g (7 oz) dried rice vermicelli
140 g (5 oz/1 cup) crushed peanuts
10 g (¼ oz/½ cup) Vietnamese mint leaves, torn
1 large handful coriander (cilantro) leaves
½ red onion, cut into thin wedges
1 green mango, cut into matchsticks
1 Lebanese (short) cucumber, halved lengthways and thinly sliced on the diagonal

LEMONGRASS DRESSING
125 ml (4 fl oz/½ cup) lime juice
1 tablespoon shaved palm sugar (jaggery)
3 tablespoons seasoned rice vinegar
2 lemongrass stems, finely chopped
2 red chillies, seeded and finely chopped
3 makrut (kaffir lime) leaves, shredded

1 Place the rice vermicelli in a bowl and cover with boiling water. Leave for 10 minutes, or until soft, then drain, rinse under cold water and cut into short lengths.

2 Place the vermicelli, three-quarters of the peanuts, the mint, coriander, onion, mango and cucumber in a large bowl and toss together.

3 To make the dressing, place all the ingredients in a screw-top jar and shake together.

4 Toss the salad and dressing and refrigerate for 30 minutes. Sprinkle with the remaining nuts to serve.

Using a sharp knife carefully cut the green mango into matchsticks.

Put the salad ingredients in a bowl and toss well, reserving some of the peanuts to garnish.

NUTRITION PER SERVE (6)
Protein 6.5 g; Fat 13 g; Carbohydrate 19 g; Dietary Fibre 3 g; Cholesterol 0 mg; 926 kJ (221 Cal)

Tomato, haloumi and spinach salad

PREPARATION TIME: 15 MINUTES + 2 HOURS MARINATING | TOTAL COOKING TIME: 1 HOUR | SERVES 4

200 g (7 oz) haloumi cheese
60 ml (2 fl oz/¼ cup) olive oil
2 garlic cloves, crushed
1 tablespoon chopped oregano
1 tablespoon chopped marjoram
4 large or 8 small roma (plum) tomatoes, halved
1 small red onion, cut into 8 wedges with base intact
3 tablespoons olive oil, extra
2 tablespoons balsamic vinegar
150 g (5½ oz) baby English spinach leaves

1 Cut the haloumi into 1 cm (½ inch) slices lengthways and put in a shallow dish. Mix together the oil, garlic and herbs and pour over the haloumi. Marinate, covered, for 1–2 hours.

2 Preheat the oven to 200°C (400°F/Gas 6). Place the tomato and onion in a single layer in a roasting tin, drizzle with 2 tablespoons of the extra olive oil and 1 tablespoon of the vinegar and sprinkle with salt and freshly ground black pepper. Bake for 50–60 minutes, or until golden.

3 Meanwhile, heat a non-stick frying pan over medium heat. Drain the haloumi and cook for 1 minute each side, or until golden brown.

4 Divide the spinach leaves among four serving plates and top with the tomato and onion. Whisk together the remaining olive oil and balsamic vinegar in a small bowl and drizzle over the salad. Top with the haloumi.

NUTRITION PER SERVE
Protein 14 g; Fat 27 g; Carbohydrate 6.5 g; Dietary Fibre 4 g; Cholesterol 26 mg; 1333 kJ (320 Cal)

Cut the red onion carefully into eight wedges, keeping the base intact.

Drain the marinated haloumi and cook for a minute on each side, until golden brown.

Wild mushroom salad

PREPARATION TIME: 15 MINUTES | TOTAL COOKING TIME: 15 MINUTES | SERVES 4

100 g (3½ oz) hazelnuts
1 mizuna lettuce
90 g (3¼ oz) baby curly endive
60 g (2¼ oz) baby English spinach
2 tablespoons hazelnut oil
2 tablespoons light olive oil
500 g (1 lb 2 oz) wild mushrooms (enoki, shimeji, shiitake, oyster)
150 g (5½ oz) strong blue cheese, crumbled

TOMATO MUSTARD VINAIGRETTE

125 ml (4 fl oz/½ cup) olive oil
2 tablespoons tarragon vinegar
½ teaspoon tomato paste (concentrated purée)
½ teaspoon dijon mustard

NUTRITION PER SERVE
Protein 10 g; Fat 75 g; Carbohydrate 20 g; Dietary Fibre 4 g; Cholesterol 40 mg; 3375 kJ (805 Cal)

1 Preheat the oven to 180°C (350°F/Gas 4). Put the hazelnuts on a baking tray and cook for 10 minutes, shaking the tray occasionally. Remove from the oven, cool, and remove the skins by rubbing the nuts together in a tea towel (dish towel). Coarsely chop the nuts.

2 Remove the tough lower stems from the mizuna and endive, and tear the larger leaves into bite-sized pieces. Wash the mizuna, endive and spinach under cold water, dry completely and refrigerate until well chilled.

3 To make the vinaigrette, whisk the ingredients together and season well.

4 Heat the oils in a frying pan and sauté the mushrooms for 3–4 minutes, or until beginning to soften. Remove from the heat and cool slightly, then stir in the vinaigrette. Arrange the salad greens on serving plates. Spoon the mushrooms over the top and sprinkle with the cheese and hazelnuts.

NOTE: *Chestnut mushrooms or chanterelles can also be used. Pink oyster mushrooms, if available, will make this salad look particularly attractive.*

Rub the hazelnuts together in a tea towel to remove the skins.

Remove the tough lower stems from the baby curly endive by snapping them off with your fingers.

Sauté the mushrooms until they are just beginning to soften.

Asparagus and mushroom salad

PREPARATION TIME: 20 MINUTES | TOTAL COOKING TIME: 10 MINUTES | SERVES 4

155 g (5½ oz) asparagus spears
1 tablespoon wholegrain mustard
3 tablespoons orange juice
2 tablespoons lemon juice
1 tablespoon lime juice
1 tablespoon orange zest
2 teaspoons lemon zest
2 teaspoons lime zest
2 garlic cloves, crushed
90 g (3¼ oz/¼ cup) honey
400 g (14 oz) button mushrooms, halved
150 g (5½ oz) rocket (arugula)
1 red capsicum (pepper), cut into strips

1 Snap the woody ends from the asparagus spears and cut in half on the diagonal. Cook in boiling water for 1 minute, or until just tender. Drain, plunge into cold water and set aside.

2 Place the mustard, citrus juice and zest, garlic and honey in a large saucepan and season with freshly ground black pepper. Bring to the boil, then reduce the heat and add the mushrooms, tossing for 2 minutes. Cool.

3 Remove the mushrooms from the sauce with a slotted spoon. Return the sauce to the heat, bring to the boil, then reduce the heat and simmer for 3–5 minutes, or until reduced and syrupy. Cool slightly.

4 Toss the mushrooms, rocket leaves, capsicum and asparagus. Put on a plate and drizzle with the sauce.

Use a zester to remove the zest of the orange, lemon and lime.

Toss the mushrooms in the mustard, juices, zest, garlic and honey.

NUTRITION PER SERVE
Protein 6 g; Fat 0 g; Carbohydrate 25 g; Dietary Fibre 5 g; Cholesterol 0 mg; 550 kJ (132 Cal)

Citrus, fennel and rocket salad

PREPARATION TIME: 25 MINUTES | TOTAL COOKING TIME: 5 MINUTES | SERVES 4

2 lemons
2 oranges
1 large fennel bulb or 2 baby fennel
200 g (7 oz) rocket (arugula)
100 g (3½ oz) pecans, chopped
90 g (3¼ oz/½ cup) stuffed green olives, halved lengthways

TOASTED SESAME DRESSING

1 tablespoon sesame oil
1 tablespoon sesame seeds
3 tablespoons olive oil
2 tablespoons white wine vinegar
1 teaspoon French mustard

1 Peel the lemons and oranges, removing all the white pith. Using a sharp knife or mandolin cut the fruit into thin slices and remove any seeds. Thinly slice the fennel. Wash and dry the rocket leaves and tear into pieces. Chill the salad while making the dressing.

2 To make the dressing, heat the sesame oil in a small saucepan over moderate heat. Add the sesame seeds and fry, stirring constantly, until lightly golden. Remove from the heat and cool. Pour the mixture into a small bowl, whisk in the remaining ingredients and season with salt and freshly ground black pepper.

3 Combine the fruit, fennel, rocket, pecans and olives in a shallow serving bowl. Drizzle with the dressing.

NOTE: *Blood oranges have a lovely tart flavour and, when in season, are delicious in this recipe.*

NUTRITION PER SERVE
Protein 6 g; Fat 40 g; Carbohydrate 10 g; Dietary Fibre 9 g; Cholesterol 0 mg; 1820 kJ (435 Cal)

Cut the peeled lemons and oranges into thin slices and remove any seeds.

Using a large, sharp knife, thinly slice the fennel bulb crossways.

Roast beetroot and onion wedge salad

PREPARATION TIME: 30 MINUTES | TOTAL COOKING TIME: 1 HOUR 30 MINUTES | SERVES 4–6

4 beetroot (beets)
3 red onions
4 tablespoons oil
20 g (¾ oz) butter
1 teaspoon ground cumin
1 teaspoon soft brown sugar
2 tablespoons orange juice
2 tablespoons orange zest

SOUR CREAM DRESSING
150 g (5½ oz) sour cream
2 tablespoons snipped chives
1 tablespoon chopped thyme
1 teaspoon lemon juice

NUTRITION PER SERVE (6)
Protein 3 g; Fat 25 g; Carbohydrate 10 g; Dietary Fibre 4 g; Cholesterol 40 mg; 1185 kJ (280 Cal)

1 Preheat the oven to 180°C (350°F/ Gas 4). Trim the leafy tops from the beetroot, leaving a short stalk, and wash thoroughly. Keep the beetroot whole to avoid bleeding during baking. Cut each onion into 6 large wedges, leaving the bases intact so the wedges hold together. Put the oil, beetroot and onion in a large baking dish and bake for 1 hour and 15 minutes. Put the beetroot and onion on separate plates and cool slightly. Peel the skins from the beetroot. Trim the tops and tails, and cut into wedges.

2 Heat the butter in a frying pan, add the cumin and brown sugar, and cook for 1 minute. Add the orange juice and simmer for 5 minutes, or until the juice has reduced slightly. Add the baked beetroot wedges and orange zest, and stir gently over low heat for 2 minutes.

3 To make the dressing, mix together the sour cream, chives, thyme and lemon juice. Arrange the cooked beetroot and onion wedges on a large plate and drizzle the dressing over the top.

Trim the leafy tops from the beetroot, leaving a short stalk on each one.

Cut the onions into wedges, leaving as much of the base intact as possible.

Add the beetroot wedges and orange zest to the pan and cook over low heat.

Greek salad

PREPARATION TIME: 20 MINUTES | TOTAL COOKING TIME: NIL | SERVES 6–8

6 tomatoes, cut into thin wedges
1 red onion, cut into thin rings
2 Lebanese (short) cucumbers, sliced
185 g (6½ oz/1 cup) kalamata olives
200 g (7 oz) feta cheese
125 ml (4 fl oz/½ cup) extra virgin olive oil
dried oregano, to sprinkle

1 Combine the tomato wedges with the onion rings, sliced cucumber and kalamata olives in a large bowl. Season to taste with salt and freshly ground black pepper.

2 Break up the feta into large pieces with your fingers and scatter over the top of the salad. Drizzle with the olive oil and sprinkle with some oregano.

NUTRITION PER SERVE (8)
Protein 6 g; Fat 25 g; Carbohydrate 3 g; Dietary Fibre 2 g; Cholesterol 15 mg; 1060 kJ (250 Cal)

Cut the tomatoes into thin wedges, and cut the red onion into thin rings.

Combine the tomato, onion, cucumber and olives in a large bowl.

Good feta should break up and crumble nicely. Just use your fingers.

Hokkien noodle salad

PREPARATION TIME: 20 MINUTES | TOTAL COOKING TIME: NIL | SERVES 8

900 g (2 lb) hokkien (egg) noodles
6 spring onions (scallions), sliced diagonally
1 large red capsicum (pepper), thinly sliced
200 g (7 oz) snow peas (mangetouts), sliced
1 carrot, cut into thin matchsticks
1 small handful mint, chopped
I small handful coriander (cilantro), chopped
100 g (3½ oz) roasted cashew nuts

SESAME DRESSING
2 teaspoons sesame oil
1 tablespoon peanut oil
2 tablespoons lime juice
2 tablespoons kecap manis (see NOTE, page 42)
3 tablespoons sweet chilli sauce

1 Gently separate the noodles and place in a large bowl, cover with boiling water and leave for 2 minutes. Rinse and drain.

2 Put the noodles in a large bowl, and add the spring onions, capsicum, snow peas, carrot, mint and coriander. Toss together well.

3 To make the dressing, whisk together the oils, lime juice, kecap manis and sweet chilli sauce. Pour the dressing over the salad and toss again. Sprinkle the cashew nuts over the top and serve immediately.

Top and tail the snow peas, then finely slice lengthways with a sharp knife.

Separate the noodles, then put them in a large bowl and cover with boiling water.

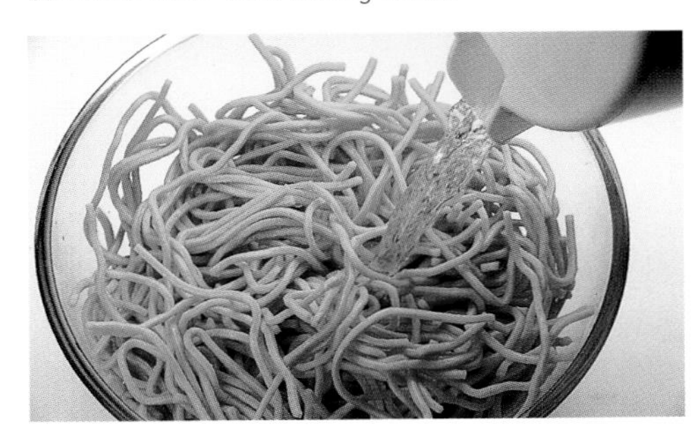

NUTRITION PER SERVE
Protein 10 g; Fat 9 g; Carbohydrate 35 g; Dietary Fibre 4.5 g; Cholesterol 0 mg; 1115 kJ (265 Cal)

Stir-fries

Potato noodles with vegetables

PREPARATION TIME: 30 MINUTES + SOAKING | TOTAL COOKING TIME: 25 MINUTES | SERVES 4

300 g (10½ oz) dried potato starch noodles
30 g (1 oz) dried cloud-ear (black) fungus
3 tablespoons sesame oil
2 tablespoons vegetable oil
3 garlic cloves, finely chopped
4 cm (1½ inch) piece of fresh ginger, grated
2 spring onions (scallions) finely chopped
2 carrots, cut into short matchsticks
2 spring onions, extra, cut into short lengths
500 g (1 lb 2 oz) baby bok choy (pak choy) or
250 g (9 oz) English spinach, roughly chopped
3 tablespoons shoshoyu (Japanese soy sauce)
2 tablespoons mirin
1 teaspoon sugar
2 tablespoons sesame seed

NUTRITION PER SERVE
Protein 5 g; Fat 11 g; Carbohydrate 20 g; Dietary Fibre 3 g; Cholesterol 0 mg; 830 kJ (198 Cal)

1 Cook the dried potato noodles in boiling water for about 5 minutes, or until translucent. Drain and then rinse under cold running water until cold. (Thoroughly rinsing the noodles will remove any excess starch.) Roughly chop the noodles into lengths of about 15 cm (6 inches), to make them easier to eat with chopsticks.

2 Pour boiling water over the fungus and soak for 10 minutes. Drain thoroughly and chop roughly. Heat 1 tablespoon of the sesame oil with the vegetable oil in a large, heavy-based pan or wok. Add the garlic, ginger and spring onion to the pan and cook for 3 minutes over medium heat, stirring regularly. Add the carrot and stir-fry for 1 minute.

3 Add the noodles, extra spring onion, bok choy, remaining sesame oil, shoshoyu, mirin and sugar. Toss well, cover and cook over low heat for 2 minutes.

4 Add the drained fungus, cover the pan and cook for another 2 minutes. Sprinkle with the sesame seed and seaweed sprinkle. Serve immediately.

NOTE: *Japanese soy sauce is lighter and sweeter than Chinese soy sauce. It is available from Asian speciality stores, along with potato starch noodles (Korean vermicelli) and cloud-ear fungus.*

Make the noodles easier to eat by roughly chopping them with kitchen scissors.

Add the noodles, spring onion, bok choy, sesame oil, shoshoyu, mirin and sugar.

Tempeh stir-fry

PREPARATION TIME: 15 MINUTES | TOTAL COOKING TIME: 15 MINUTES | SERVES 4

1 teaspoon sesame oil
1 tablespoon peanut oil
2 garlic cloves, crushed
1 tablespoon grated fresh ginger
1 red chilli, finely sliced
4 spring onions (scallions), sliced on the diagonal
300 g (10½ oz) tempeh, diced
500 g (1 lb 2 oz) baby bok choy (pak choy) leaves
800 g (1 lb 12 oz) Chinese broccoli, chopped
125 ml (4 fl oz/½ cup) oyster sauce
2 tablespoons rice vinegar
2 tablespoons coriander (cilantro) leaves
3 tablespoons toasted cashew nuts

1 Heat the oils in a wok over high heat, add the garlic, ginger, chilli and spring onion and cook for 1–2 minutes, or until the onion is soft. Add the tempeh and cook for 5 minutes, or until golden. Remove and keep warm.

2 Add half the greens and 1 tablespoon water to the wok and cook, covered, for 3–4 minutes, or until wilted. Remove and repeat with the remaining greens and more water.

3 Return the greens and tempeh to the wok, add the sauce and vinegar and warm through. Top with the coriander and nuts. Serve with rice.

Stir-fry the garlic, ginger, chilli and spring onion for 1–2 minutes.

Add the tempeh to the wok and stir-fry for 5 minutes, or until golden.

NUTRITION PER SERVE
Protein 23 g; Fat 15 g; Carbohydrate 12 g; Dietary Fibre 15 g; Cholesterol 0 mg; 2220 kJ (529 Cal)

Tamari roasted almonds with spicy green beans

PREPARATION TIME: 10 MINUTES | TOTAL COOKING TIME: 25 MINUTES | SERVES 4–6

1 tablespoon sesame oil
500 g (1 lb 2 oz/2½ cups) jasmine rice
2 tablespoons sesame oil, extra
1 long red chilli, seeded and finely chopped
2 cm (¾ inch) piece of fresh ginger, peeled and grated
2 garlic cloves, crushed
400 g (14 oz) green beans, cut into short lengths
125 ml (4 fl oz/½ cup) hoisin sauce
1 tablespoon soft brown sugar
2 tablespoons mirin
250 g (9 oz) tamari roasted almonds, roughly chopped (see NOTE)

1 Preheat the oven to 200°C (400°F/Gas 6). Heat the oil in a 1.5 litre (52 fl oz/6 cup) ovenproof dish. Add the rice and stir to coat with oil. Stir in 1 litre (35 fl oz/4 cups) boiling water. Cover and bake for 20 minutes, or until all the water is absorbed. Keep warm.

2 Meanwhile, heat the extra oil in a wok or large frying pan and cook the chilli, ginger and garlic for 1 minute, or until lightly browned. Add the beans, hoisin sauce and sugar and stir-fry for 2 minutes. Stir in the mirin and cook for 1 minute, or until the beans are tender but still crunchy.

3 Remove from the heat and stir in the almonds. Serve on a bed of the rice.

NOTE: *Tamari roasted almonds are available from health-food stores.*

NUTRITION PER SERVE (6)
Protein 15 g; Fat 34 g; Carbohydrate 80 g; Dietary Fibre 9.5 g; Cholesterol 0 mg; 2874 kJ (687 Cal)

When chopping chillies, it's a good idea to wear disposable rubber gloves to prevent chilli burns.

Stir-fry the beans for 2 minutes, tossing to coat them in the sauce.

Asian greens and mushrooms stir-fry

PREPARATION TIME: 20 MINUTES | TOTAL COOKING TIME: 5 MINUTES | SERVES 4

- 20 stems Chinese broccoli
- 4 baby bok choy (pak choy)
- 100 g (3½ oz) shimeji or enoki mushrooms
- 100 g (3½ oz) shiitake mushrooms
- 1 tablespoon soy sauce
- 2 teaspoons crushed palm sugar (jaggery)
- 1 tablespoon oil
- 4 spring onions (scallions), cut into short pieces
- 5 cm (2 inch) fresh ginger, cut into thin strips
- 1–2 small red chillies, seeded and finely chopped, plus extra red chilli, shredded, to serve
- 2–3 garlic cloves, crushed
- 125 g (4½ oz) snow peas (mangetouts), halved
- 1–2 teaspoons dark soy sauce

1 Remove any tough outer leaves from the Chinese broccoli and bok choy. Cut into 4 cm (1½ inch) pieces across the leaves, including the stems. Wash thoroughly, then drain and dry thoroughly. Wipe the mushrooms with a paper towel and trim the ends. Slice the shiitake mushrooms thickly.

2 Combine the soy sauce and palm sugar with 3 tablespoons of water. Set aside.

3 Heat the wok until very hot, add the oil and swirl it around to coat the side. Stir-fry the spring onion, ginger, chilli and garlic over low heat for 30 seconds, without browning. Increase the heat to high and add the Chinese broccoli, bok choy and snow peas. Stir-fry for 1–2 minutes, or until the vegetables are wilted.

4 Add the prepared mushrooms and soy sauce mixture. Stir-fry over high heat for 1–2 minutes, or until the mushrooms and sauce are heated through. Sprinkle with the dark soy sauce, to taste, and serve immediately, garnished with the extra chilli.

NUTRITION PER SERVE
Protein 6.5 g; Fat 10 g; Carbohydrate 15 g; Dietary Fibre 3 g; Cholesterol 0 mg; 780 kJ (185 Cal)

You will need to gently separate the shimeji mushrooms from each other.

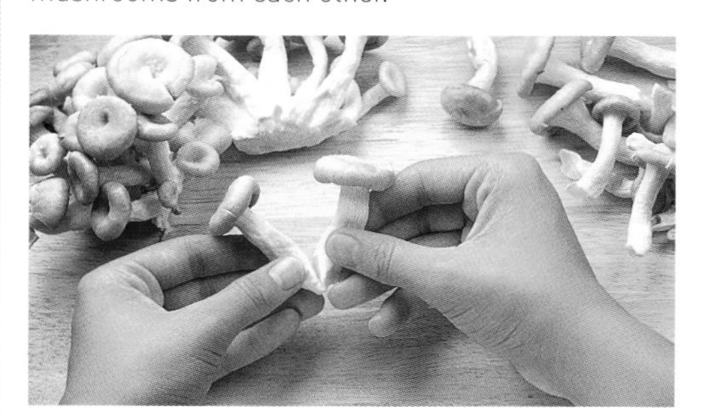

Trim the shiitake mushrooms and cut them into thick slices.

Peel the piece of ginger with a vegetable peeler or sharp knife and cut it into thin strips.

Spicy broccoli and cauliflower stir-fry

PREPARATION TIME: 15 MINUTES | TOTAL COOKING TIME: 10 MINUTES | SERVES 4

1 teaspoon ground cumin
1 teaspoon ground coriander
2 tablespoons oil
2 garlic cloves, crushed
1 teaspoon grated fresh ginger
½ teaspoon chilli powder
1 onion, cut into wedges
200 g (7 oz) cauliflower, cut into bite-sized florets
200 g (7 oz) broccoli, cut into bite-sized florets
200 g (7 oz) haloumi cheese, diced
1 tablespoon lemon juice

1 Heat the wok until very hot, add the cumin and coriander, and dry-fry the spices for 1 minute. Add the oil with the garlic, ginger and chilli powder, and stir-fry briefly. Add the onion and cook for 2–3 minutes, being careful not to burn the spices.

2 Add the cauliflower and broccoli, and stir-fry until they are cooked through but still crisp. Add the haloumi and toss well until the haloumi is coated with the spices and is just beginning to melt. Season well and serve sprinkled generously with lemon juice.

NUTRITION PER SERVE
Protein 12 g; Fat 15 g; Carbohydrate 3 g; Dietary Fibre 4 g; Cholesterol 20 mg; 820 kJ (195 Cal)

Haloumi cheese comes in a block—cut it into small, even cubes.

Dry-fry the ground cumin and coriander in a very hot wok.

Add the onion wedges to the spice mixture and toss to coat.

Sweet and sour tofu with noodles

PREPARATION TIME: 10 MINUTES | TOTAL COOKING TIME: 5 MINUTES | SERVES 4

100 g (3½ oz) deep-fried tofu puffs (see NOTE)
2 tablespoons oil
1 onion, sliced
1 red capsicum (pepper), cut into squares
3 garlic cloves, crushed
2 teaspoons grated fresh ginger
500 g (1 lb 2 oz) thin hokkien (egg) noodles, gently separated
120 g (4 oz/¾ cup) small chunks pineapple
3 tablespoons pineapple juice
3 tablespoons hoisin sauce
1 large handful roughly chopped coriander (cilantro), plus extra, to sprinkle

1 Slice the tofu puffs into three, then cut each slice into two or three pieces.

2 Heat the wok until very hot, add the oil and stir-fry the onion and capsicum for 1–2 minutes, or until beginning to soften. Add the garlic and ginger, stir-fry for 1 minute, then add the tofu and stir-fry for 2 minutes.

3 Add the noodles and pineapple chunks and toss until the mixture is combined and heated through. Add the pineapple juice, hoisin sauce and chopped coriander. Toss well. Serve immediately, sprinkled with coriander.

NOTE: *Deep-fried tofu puffs are available from the refrigerated section in Asian grocery stores and some supermarkets. They have a very different texture to ordinary tofu.*

NUTRITION PER SERVE
Protein 10 g; Fat 15 g; Carbohydrate 65 g; Dietary Fibre 3.5 g; Cholesterol 0 mg; 1830 kJ (435 Cal)

Use your fingers to gently pull apart the strands of Hokkien noodles before use.

Buy deep-fried tofu puffs, not silken tofu. Slice each tofu puff into three, then cut into pieces.

Asparagus and mustard stir-fry

PREPARATION TIME: 10 MINUTES | TOTAL COOKING TIME: 10 MINUTES | SERVES 2

480 g (1 lb 1 oz) asparagus
1 tablespoon oil
1 red onion, sliced
1 garlic clove, crushed
1 tablespoon wholegrain mustard
1 teaspoon honey
125 ml (4 fl oz/½ cup) pouring (whipping) cream

1 Break the woody ends off the asparagus by holding both ends of the spear and bending gently until it snaps. Cut the asparagus into 5 cm (2 inch) lengths.

2 Heat the wok until very hot, add the oil and swirl to coat the side. Stir-fry the onion for 2–3 minutes, or until tender. Stir in the crushed garlic and cook for 1 minute. Add the asparagus to the wok and stir-fry for 3–4 minutes, or until tender, being careful not to overcook the asparagus.

3 Remove the asparagus from the wok, set it aside and keep warm. Combine the wholegrain mustard, honey and cream. Add to the wok and bring to the boil, then reduce the heat and simmer for 2–3 minutes, or until the mixture reduces and thickens slightly. Return the asparagus to the wok and toss it through the cream mixture. Serve immediately.

VARIATION: *When asparagus is in season, white and purple asparagus are also available. Vary the recipe by using a mixture of the three colours. Do not overcook the purple asparagus or it will turn green as it cooks.*

HINT: *This dish can also be served on croutons, toasted ciabatta or toasted wholegrain bread as a smart starter or first course.*

NUTRITION PER SERVE
Protein 8.5 g; Fat 35 g; Carbohydrate 10 g; Dietary Fibre 5 g; Cholesterol 85 mg; 1685 kJ (405 Cal)

Gently bend the asparagus spear and the tough woody end will naturally snap off.

Stir-fry the sliced red onion for 2–3 minutes, or until tender.

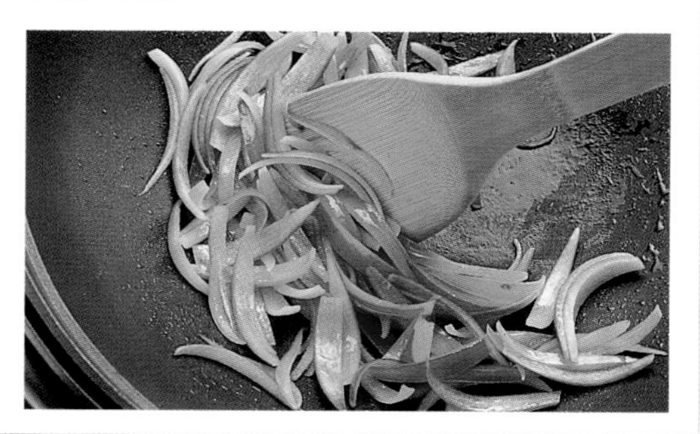

Pumpkin and cashew stir-fry

PREPARATION TIME: 20 MINUTES | TOTAL COOKING TIME: 15 MINUTES | SERVES 4–6

oil, for cooking
5½ oz (155 g/1 cup) raw cashews
1 leek, white part only, sliced
2 teaspoons ground coriander
2 teaspoons ground cumin
2 teaspoons brown mustard seeds
2 garlic cloves, crushed
1 kg (2 lb 4 oz) butternut pumpkin (squash), cubed
185 ml (6 fl oz/¾ cup) orange juice
1 teaspoon soft brown sugar

1 Heat the wok until very hot, add 1 tablespoon of the oil and swirl to coat. Stir-fry the cashews until golden, then drain on paper towels. Stir-fry the leek for 2–3 minutes, or until softened. Remove from the wok.

2 Reheat the wok, add 1 tablespoon of the oil and stir-fry the coriander, cumin, mustard seeds and garlic for 2 minutes, or until the mustard seeds begin to pop. Add the pumpkin and stir to coat well. Stir-fry for 5 minutes, or until the pumpkin is brown and tender.

3 Add the orange juice and sugar. Bring to the boil and cook for 5 minutes. Add the leek and three-quarters of the cashews and toss well. Top with the remaining cashews.

NUTRITION PER SERVE (6)
Protein 8 g; Fat 20 g; Carbohydrate 20 g; Dietary Fibre 4 g; Cholesterol 0 mg; 1240 kJ (295 Cal)

Stir-fry the cashews in 1 tablespoon of the oil until they are golden.

Reheat the wok and stir-fry the coriander, cumin, mustard seeds and garlic.

Add the pumpkin and stir to coat well in the spices. Stir-fry until brown and tender.

Three-bean stir-fry

PREPARATION TIME: 10 MINUTES | TOTAL COOKING TIME: 5 MINUTES | SERVES 4

1 tablespoon oil
1 red onion, chopped
2 garlic cloves, crushed
1 tablespoon finely chopped thyme
200 g (7 oz) green beans, cut into short lengths
300 g (10½ oz) tin cannellini beans, rinsed
170 g (5¾ oz/1 cup) chickpeas, drained and rinsed
150 g (5½ oz) rocket (arugula)
2 tablespoons finely chopped parsley
3 tablespoons lemon juice

1 Heat the wok until very hot, add the oil and swirl it around to coat the side. Stir-fry the onion for 2 minutes. Add the garlic and stir-fry until soft. Stir in the thyme.

2 Add the green beans and stir-fry for 2–3 minutes, or until tender. Add the cannellini beans and chickpeas, and stir-fry until heated through. Season, and spoon the mixture onto the rocket on a platter. Sprinkle the parsley on top and drizzle with the lemon juice to serve.

NUTRITION PER SERVE
Protein 7 g; Fat 6 g; Carbohydrate 10 g; Dietary Fibre 6.5 g; Cholesterol 0 mg; 530 kJ (125 Cal)

Add the green beans to the onion, garlic and thyme, and stir-fry until tender.

Crisp tofu in a hot bean sauce

PREPARATION TIME: 35 MINUTES + 30 MINUTES MARINATING | TOTAL COOKING TIME: 15 MINUTES | SERVES 4

500 g (1 lb 2 oz) firm tofu, cut into small cubes
2 tablespoons peanut oil
3 tablespoons soy sauce
2 teaspoons finely grated fresh ginger
oil, for cooking
125 g (4 oz/¾ cup) rice flour
2 onions, cut into thin wedges
2 garlic cloves, finely chopped
2 teaspoons soft brown sugar
½ red capsicum (pepper), cut into short, thin strips
5 spring onions (scallions), cut into short pieces
2 tablespoons dry sherry
2 teaspoons finely grated orange zest
2 tablespoons hot bean paste

1 Place the tofu in a non-metallic bowl with the peanut oil. Add the soy sauce and ginger, cover and refrigerate for 30 minutes.

2 Drain the tofu, reserving the marinade, and toss several pieces at a time in the rice flour to coat heavily. Heat the wok until very hot, add about 3 tablespoons of the oil and swirl it around to coat the side. Add the tofu to the hot oil and stir-fry over medium heat for 1½ minutes, or until golden all over. Remove from the wok and drain on paper towels. Repeat with the remaining tofu. Keep warm. Drain any oil from the wok.

3 Reheat the wok and stir-fry the onion, garlic and sugar for 3 minutes, or until golden. Add the capsicum, spring onion, sherry, orange zest, bean paste and the reserved tofu marinade. Stir and bring to the boil. Return the tofu to the wok, toss to heat through, and serve.

NUTRITION PER SERVE
Protein 15 g; Fat 8 g; Carbohydrate 40 g; Dietary Fibre 3 g; Cholesterol 0 mg; 1215 kJ (290 Cal)

Marinate the tofu in the peanut oil and soy sauce, including the ginger, for 30 minutes before cooking.

Drain the tofu in a sieve, then toss it in the rice flour to coat heavily.

Stir-fry the tofu until it is golden on all sides, then drain on paper towels.

Green beans with shiitake mushrooms

PREPARATION TIME: 15 MINUTES | TOTAL COOKING TIME: 12 MINUTES | SERVES 4 AS A MAIN COURSE, OR 6–8 AS AN ACCOMPANIMENT

2 tablespoons sesame seeds
1 tablespoon oil
1 teaspoon sesame oil
5 spring onions (scallions), sliced
800 g (1 lb 12 oz) green beans
200 g (7 oz) shiitake mushrooms, halved or quartered
2 teaspoons finely chopped fresh ginger
2 tablespoons mirin
2 tablespoons soy sauce
1 tablespoon sugar

1 Heat the wok until very hot, add the sesame seeds and dry-fry for 2–3 minutes over high heat, or until they are golden. Remove from the wok and set aside.

2 Reheat the wok, add the oils and swirl to coat the side. Add the spring onion and beans, and stir-fry for 4 minutes. Add the mushrooms and ginger, and cook for 4 minutes.

3 Pour in the mirin, soy sauce and sugar, cover and cook for 2 minutes, or until the beans are tender. Sprinkle with the toasted sesame seeds.

NUTRITION PER SERVE (4)
Protein 7.5 g; Fat 12 g; Carbohydrate 10 g; Dietary Fibre 7 g; Cholesterol 0 mg; 885 kJ (210 Cal)

Peel the fresh ginger and chop it finely to make up 2 teaspoons.

Dry-fry the sesame seeds over high heat until they are golden.

Stir-fry the spring onion and beans in the oil and sesame oil.

Stir-fried eggplant with lemon

PREPARATION TIME: 20 MINUTES + 30 MINUTES STANDING | TOTAL COOKING TIME: 12 MINUTES | SERVES 4

1 kg (2 lb 4 oz) small eggplants (aubergines)
olive oil, for cooking
8 spring onions (scallions), sliced
3 garlic cloves, crushed
2 teaspoons cumin seeds
1 tablespoon ground coriander
1 teaspoon grated lemon zest
4 tablespoons lemon juice
2 teaspoons soft brown sugar
2 tablespoons coriander (cilantro) leaves

1 Peel the eggplants and cut into small cubes. Put in a colander and sprinkle with 1 tablespoon of salt. Leave for 30 minutes, then rinse under cold water and pat dry with paper towels.

2 Heat the wok until very hot, add 1½ tablespoons of the oil and swirl it around to coat the side. Stir-fry the eggplant in two batches over high heat for 3–4 minutes, or until browned and cooked (use 1½ tablespoons oil for each batch). Remove from the wok.

3 Return all the eggplant to the wok and add the spring onion. Stir-fry for 1 minute, or until the eggplant is soft. Add the garlic and cumin seeds, and cook for 1 minute. Stir in the ground coriander and cook for 30 seconds. Add the lemon zest, lemon juice and sugar, and toss well. Season with salt and freshly ground black pepper and sprinkle with coriander leaves. Delicious served with buckwheat (soba) noodles.

NUTRITION PER SERVE
Protein 3.5 g; Fat 10 g; Carbohydrate 10 g; Dietary Fibre 7 g; Cholesterol 0 mg; 640 kJ (155 Cal)

Grate the lemon zest on the fine side of a metal grater, avoiding the bitter pith underneath.

Stir-fry the eggplant in batches until it is browned and cooked through.

Sesame tofu stir-fry

PREPARATION TIME: 20 MINUTES + 30 MINUTES MARINATING | TOTAL COOKING TIME: 10 MINUTES | SERVES 4

300 g (10½ oz) hard tofu
2 teaspoons sesame oil
2 tablespoons soy sauce
1 tablespoon sesame seeds
2 tablespoons oil
3 zucchini (courgettes), sliced
150 g (5½ oz) button mushrooms, halved or quartered
1 large red capsicum (pepper), cut into squares
2 garlic cloves, crushed
550 g (1 lb 4 oz/3 cups) cold, cooked brown rice
1–2 tablespoons soy sauce, extra

1 Drain the tofu and pat dry with paper towels. Cut into cubes, place in a non-metallic bowl and add the sesame oil and soy sauce. Stir well and leave in the fridge to marinate for 30 minutes, stirring occasionally.

2 Heat the wok until very hot, add the sesame seeds and dry-fry for 2–3 minutes, or until lightly golden. Tip onto a plate to cool.

3 Reheat the wok, add the oil and swirl it around to coat the side. Remove the tofu from the dish with a slotted spoon and reserve the marinade. Stir-fry the tofu over high heat, turning occasionally, for about 3 minutes, or until browned. Remove from the wok and set aside.

4 Add the vegetables and garlic, and cook, stirring often, until they are just tender. Add the rice and tofu, and stir-fry until heated through.

5 Add the toasted sesame seeds, the reserved marinade and extra soy sauce to taste. Toss to coat the tofu and vegetables, then serve immediately.

Dry-fry the sesame seeds until they are lightly golden brown.

NUTRITION PER SERVE
Protein 15 g; Fat 20 g; Carbohydrate 50 g; Dietary Fibre 5.5 g; Cholesterol 0 mg; 1815 kJ (435 Cal)

Chilli noodle and nut stir-fry

PREPARATION TIME: 20 MINUTES | TOTAL COOKING TIME: 12 MINUTES | SERVES 4

1½ tablespoons oil
1 tablespoon sesame oil
2–3 small red chillies, finely chopped
1 large onion, cut into thin wedges
4 garlic cloves, very thinly sliced
1 red capsicum (pepper), cut into strips
1 green capsicum (pepper), cut into strips
2 large carrots, cut into matchsticks
100 g (3½ oz) green beans
2 celery stalks, cut into matchsticks
2 teaspoons honey
500 g (1 lb 2 oz) hokkien (egg) noodles, gently separated
100 g (3½ oz) dry-roasted peanuts
100 g (3½ oz) honey-roast cashew nuts
4 tablespoons snipped garlic chives, or 4 spring onions (scallions), chopped
sweet chilli sauce and sesame oil, to serve

1 Heat the wok over low heat, add the oils and swirl them to coat the side. When the oil is warm, add the chilli and heat until the oil is very hot.

2 Add the onion and garlic, and stir-fry for 1 minute, or until the onion just softens. Add the capsicum, carrot and beans, and stir-fry for 1 minute. Add the celery, honey and 1 tablespoon water, and season with salt and freshly ground black pepper. Toss well, then cover and cook for 1–2 minutes, or until the vegetables are just tender.

3 Add the noodles and nuts and toss well. Cook, covered, for 1–2 minutes, or until the noodles are heated through. Stir in the garlic chives and serve, drizzled with the sweet chilli sauce and sesame oil.

Peel the cloves of garlic, then cut them into paper-thin slices.

Heat the oil until warm, then add the chilli and heat until the oil is very hot.

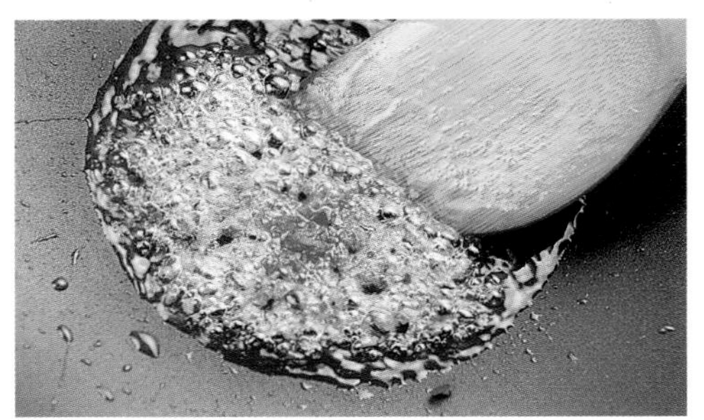

NUTRITION PER SERVE
Protein 20 g; Fat 45 g; Carbohydrate 75 g; Dietary Fibre 7 g; Cholesterol 0 mg; 3330 kJ (795 Cal)

Fragrant greens

PREPARATION TIME: 15 MINUTES | TOTAL COOKING TIME: 8 MINUTES | SERVES 4

2 tablespoons oil
300 g (10½ oz) broccoli, cut into small florets
150 g (5½ oz) snake (yard-long) beans, cut into short lengths
3 spring onions (scallions), sliced
250 g (9 oz) cabbage, finely shredded
1 green capsicum (pepper), cut into strips
2 tablespoons lime juice
1 tablespoon soft brown sugar
2 small handfuls Thai basil, shredded (see NOTE)

1 Heat the wok until very hot, add the oil and swirl it around to coat the side. Stir-fry the broccoli and snake beans for 3–4 minutes, or until the vegetables are bright green and just tender. Add the spring onion, cabbage and capsicum, and continue stir-frying until just softened.

2 Combine the lime juice and brown sugar, stirring until the sugar has dissolved. Add to the wok with the basil. Toss to combine with the vegetables and serve immediately.

NOTE: *You can include any suitable kind of green vegetable in this dish, including Asian greens. If you can't find Thai basil, use ordinary basil or coriander (cilantro)—either will give fragrance and flavour like Thai basil.*

Using a large sharp knife, finely shred the cabbage so that it will stir-fry quickly.

Shred the Thai basil just before you need it, or it will turn black.

NUTRITION PER SERVE
Protein 6 g; Fat 10 g; Carbohydrate 9 g; Dietary Fibre 7 g; Cholesterol 0 mg; 630 kJ (150 Cal)

Stir-fried tofu with orange and fresh pineapple

PREPARATION TIME: 35 MINUTES | TOTAL COOKING TIME: 10 MINUTES | SERVES 4

250 g (9 oz) firm tofu, cut into cubes
5 cm (2 inch) fresh ginger, grated
2 teaspoons finely grated orange zest
oil, for cooking
2 large onions, cut into thin wedges
3 garlic cloves, finely chopped
2 teaspoons soft brown sugar
2 teaspoons white vinegar
250 g (9 oz) fresh pineapple, cut into bite-sized pieces
1 tablespoon orange juice

NUTRITION PER SERVE
Protein 6.5 g; Fat 3 g; Carbohydrate 15 g; Dietary Fibre 3 g; Cholesterol 0 mg; 430 kJ (100 Cal)

1 Put the tofu, ginger, orange zest and some freshly ground black pepper in a non-metallic bowl. Stir, cover and refrigerate.

2 Heat the wok until very hot, add 1½ tablespoons of the oil and swirl it around to coat the side. Stir-fry the onion, garlic and brown sugar over medium heat for 2–3 minutes, or until the onion is soft and golden. Stir in the vinegar and cook for 2 minutes. Remove from the wok.

3 Reheat the wok and add the pineapple and orange juice. Stir-fry for 3 minutes over high heat, or until the pineapple is just soft and golden. Stir in the onion mixture, remove from the wok, cover and set aside.

4 Reheat the wok until very hot and add 1½ tablespoons of the oil. Stir-fry the tofu in two batches, tossing regularly until it is lightly crisp and golden. Drain on paper towels.

5 Return the tofu and the pineapple mixture to the wok, and toss to heat through. Season well and serve.

Drain the firm tofu, and cut it into bite-sized cubes with a sharp knife.

Stir-fry the onion, garlic and brown sugar until the onion is soft and golden.

Stir-fry the marinated tofu in two batches until it is lightly crisp and golden.

Stir-fried cauliflower with toasted nuts

PREPARATION TIME: 30 MINUTES | TOTAL COOKING TIME: 20 MINUTES | SERVES 4

2 tablespoons oil
2 tablespoons mild curry paste
1 tablespoon currants
1 tablespoon grated fresh ginger
4 spring onions (scallions), diagonally sliced
500 g (1 lb 2 oz) cauliflower, cut into bite-sized florets
2 teaspoons sesame oil
150 g (5½ oz) walnuts, toasted
150 g (5½ oz) cashew nuts, toasted
1 tablespoon sesame seeds

1 Heat the wok until very hot, add the oil and swirl it around to coat the side. Stir-fry the curry paste for 3 minutes, or until fragrant. Add the currants, ginger, spring onion and cauliflower. Stir-fry for 4–5 minutes, adding about 80 ml (2½ fl oz/⅓ cup) water to moisten. Cover and steam for 1–2 minutes, or until the cauliflower is tender.

2 Season with salt and freshly ground black pepper, and drizzle with the sesame oil. Toss the toasted walnuts and cashew nuts through the cauliflower mixture. Serve sprinkled with the sesame seeds.

NUTRITION PER SERVE
Protein 15 g; Fat 60 g; Carbohydrate 10 g; Dietary Fibre 8 g; Cholesterol 0 mg; 2750 kJ (655 Cal)

Toast the walnuts and cashew nuts by dry-frying them in the wok.

Heat the oil in the very hot wok and stir-fry the curry paste until it is fragrant.

Add the currants, ginger, spring onion and cauliflower, and toss well.

Wild mushrooms with spices

PREPARATION TIME: 30 MINUTES | TOTAL COOKING TIME: 5 MINUTES | SERVE 4

20 g (¾ oz) butter
1 tablespoon oil
2 garlic cloves, crushed
1 teaspoon ground cumin
1 teaspoon ground coriander
¼ teaspoon sweet paprika
750 g (1 lb 10 oz) mixed mushrooms (see NOTE), cleaned and trimmed
2 tablespoons dry sherry
4 spring onions (scallions), sliced
2 small handfuls shredded fresh basil
2 tablespoons chopped fresh flat-leaf (Italian) parsley

1 Heat the wok until very hot, add the butter and oil and swirl it around to coat the side. Stir-fry the garlic, cumin, coriander and paprika for 1–2 minutes, or until fragrant. Add the mushrooms and stir-fry for 2 minutes.

2 Add the sherry and bring to the boil. Cover and cook for 30 seconds. Toss the spring onion and herbs through the mushroom mixture. Serve with rice or noodles as a main dish.

NOTE: *Mushrooms such as shimeji, oyster, Swiss brown, enoki and button can be used in this recipe. If using enoki mushrooms, add them when the sherry is added as they cook faster than the other mushrooms.*

Clean and trim the mushrooms, cutting any larger ones in half.

Add the sherry and enoki mushrooms, and cover and cook for 2 minutes.

NUTRITION PER SERVE
Protein 7 g; Fat 9.5 g; Carbohydrate 4 g; Dietary Fibre 5.5 g; Cholesterol 15 mg; 580 kJ (140 Cal)

Grains, pulses and tofu

Tofu burgers

PREPARATION TIME: 25 MINUTES + 30 MINUTES REFRIGERATION | TOTAL COOKING TIME: 30 MINUTES | SERVES 6

1 tablespoon olive oil
1 red onion, finely chopped
200 g (7 oz) Swiss brown mushrooms, finely chopped
350 g (11 oz) hard tofu (see NOTE)
2 large garlic cloves
3 tablespoons chopped basil
200 g (7 oz/2 cups) dry wholemeal (whole-wheat) breadcrumbs
1 egg, lightly beaten
2 tablespoons balsamic vinegar
2 tablespoons sweet chilli sauce
150 g (5½ oz/1½ cups) dry wholemeal (whole-wheat) breadcrumbs, extra
olive oil, for shallow-frying
6 white or wholegrain bread rolls
125 g (4 oz/½ cup) mayonnaise
100 g (3½ oz) semi-dried (sun-blushed) tomatoes
60 g (2¼ oz) rocket (arugula) leaves
sweet chilli sauce, to serve

NUTRITION PER SERVE
Protein 23 g; Fat 24 g; Carbohydrate 86 g; Dietary Fibre 10 g; Cholesterol 37 mg; 2740 kJ (653 Cal)

1 Heat the oil in a frying pan and cook the onion over medium heat for 2–3 minutes, or until soft. Add the mushrooms and cook for a further 2 minutes. Cool slightly.

2 Blend 250 g (9 oz) of the tofu with the garlic and basil in a food processor until smooth. Transfer to a large bowl and stir in the onion mixture, breadcrumbs, egg, vinegar and sweet chilli sauce. Grate the remaining tofu and fold through the mixture, then refrigerate for 30 minutes. Divide the mixture into six and form into patties, pressing together well. Coat them in the extra breadcrumbs.

3 Heat 1 cm (½ inch) of oil in a deep frying pan and cook the patties in two batches for 4–5 minutes each side, or until golden. Turn carefully to prevent them breaking up. Drain on crumpled paper towels and season with salt.

4 Halve the bread rolls and toast under a hot grill (broiler). Spread mayonnaise over both sides of each roll. Layer a tofu patty, semi-dried tomatoes and rocket leaves on each roll and drizzle with sweet chilli sauce.

NOTE: *Hard tofu (not to be confused with 'firm' tofu) is quite rubbery and firm and won't break up during cooking. It's perfect for patties, stir-frying and pan-frying.*

Mix the tofu, garlic and basil in a food processor until smooth.

Grate the remaining hard tofu and fold it into the mixture. Refrigerate for 30 minutes.

Be careful when you turn the patties during frying. You don't want them to break up.

Green pilau with cashew nuts

PREPARATION TIME: 15 MINUTES | TOTAL COOKING TIME: 1 HOUR 10 MINUTES | SERVES 6

200 g (7 oz) baby English spinach
100 g (3½ oz/⅔ cup) cashew nuts, chopped
2 tablespoons olive oil
6 spring onions (scallions), chopped
300 g (10½ oz/1½ cups) long-grain brown rice
2 garlic cloves, finely chopped
1 teaspoon fennel seeds
2 tablespoons lemon juice
625 ml (21½ fl oz/2½ cups) vegetable stock
3 tablespoons chopped mint
3 tablespoons chopped flat-leaf (Italian) parsley

1 Preheat the oven to 180°C (350°F/Gas 4). Shred the English spinach leaves.

2 Place the cashew nuts on a baking tray and roast for 5–10 minutes, or until golden brown—watch carefully.

3 Heat the oil in a large frying pan and cook the spring onion over medium heat for 2 minutes, or until soft. Add the rice, garlic and fennel seeds and cook, stirring frequently, for 1–2 minutes, or until the rice is evenly coated. Increase the heat to high, add the lemon juice, stock and 1 teaspoon of salt and bring to the boil. Reduce to low, cover and cook for 45 minutes without lifting the lid.

4 Remove from the heat and sprinkle with the spinach and herbs. Leave, covered, for 8 minutes, then fork the spinach and herbs through the rice. Season. Serve sprinkled with the cashew nuts.

Wash the spinach thoroughly, trim away any stalks and shred the leaves.

Fork the spinach and herbs through the rice and sprinkle with cashew nuts to serve.

NUTRITION PER SERVE
Protein 6 g; Fat 12 g; Carbohydrate 32 g; Dietary Fibre 3.5 g; Cholesterol 0 mg; 1091 kJ (260 Cal)

Thai tempeh

PREPARATION TIME: 15 MINUTES + OVERNIGHT MARINATING | TOTAL COOKING TIME: 20 MINUTES | SERVES 4

THAI MARINADE
2 stems lemongrass, finely chopped
2 makrut (kaffir lime) leaves, shredded
2 small red chillies, seeded and finely chopped
3 garlic cloves, crushed
2 teaspoons sesame oil
125 ml (4 fl oz/½ cup) lime juice
2 teaspoons shaved palm sugar (jaggery)
125 ml (4 fl oz/½ cup) soy sauce

600 g (1 lb 5 oz) tofu tempeh, cut into eight 5 mm (¼ inch) slices
3 tablespoons peanut oil
1 tablespoon shaved palm sugar (jaggery)
100 g (3½ oz) snow pea (mangetout) sprouts or watercress, trimmed
makrut (kaffir lime) leaves, finely shredded

1 To make the Thai marinade, mix the lemongrass, makrut leaves, chilli, garlic, sesame oil, lime juice, palm sugar and soy sauce in a non-metallic bowl. Add the tempeh. Cover and marinate overnight in the fridge, turning occasionally.

2 Drain the tempeh, reserving the marinade. Heat half the peanut oil in a frying pan over high heat. Cook the tempeh in batches, turning once, for 5 minutes, or until crisp, adding more oil when needed. Drain on paper towels. Heat the reserved marinade with the palm sugar in a saucepan until syrupy.

3 Put a slice of tempeh on each serving plate and top with some snow pea sprouts. Repeat, finishing with the snow pea sprouts on top. Drizzle with the reserved marinade and sprinkle with makrut leaves.

NUTRITION PER SERVE
Protein 9.5 g; Fat 20 g; Carbohydrate 7 g; Dietary Fibre 1.5 g; Cholesterol 0 mg; 1102 kJ (262 Cal)

Cook the slices of tempeh in batches, turning once, until they are crisp.

Heat the reserved marinade and palm sugar in a saucepan until the mixture is syrupy.

Couscous vegetable loaf

PREPARATION TIME: 20 MINUTES + COOLING + OVERNIGHT REFRIGERATION | TOTAL COOKING TIME: 10 MINUTES | SERVES 6

500 ml (17 fl oz/2 cups) vegetable stock
250 g (9 oz) instant couscous
15 g (½ oz) butter
1½ tablespoons olive oil
1 garlic clove, crushed
1 small onion, finely chopped
2 teaspoons ground coriander
½ teaspoon ground cinnamon
½ teaspoon garam masala
125 g (4½ oz) cherry tomatoes, quartered
1 small zucchini (courgette), diced
65 g (2½ oz) tin corn kernels, drained and rinsed
8 large basil leaves
70 g (2½ oz) sun-dried capsicums (peppers) in oil
1 large handful chopped basil

DRESSING
4 tablespoons orange juice
1 tablespoon lemon juice
3 tablespoons chopped flat-leaf (Italian) parsley
1 teaspoon honey
1 teaspoon ground cumin

1 Bring the stock to the boil. Put the couscous and butter in a bowl, cover with the stock; leave for 10 minutes.

2 Heat 1 tablespoon of the oil in a large frying pan and cook the garlic and onion over low heat for 5 minutes, or until the onion is soft. Add the spices and cook for 1 minute, or until fragrant. Remove from the pan.

3 Add the remaining oil to the pan and cook the tomatoes, zucchini and corn over high heat until soft.

4 Line a 2 litre (70 fl oz/8 cup) loaf tin with plastic wrap, letting it overhang the sides. Arrange the basil leaves in the base of the tin. Drain the capsicums, reserving 2 tablespoons of the oil, then roughly chop. Add the onion mixture, tomato mixture, capsicum and chopped basil to the couscous and mix. Cool.

5 Press into the tin and fold the plastic wrap over to cover. Weigh down with cans of food to compress the loaf and refrigerate overnight.

6 To make the dressing, put all the ingredients and reserved capsicum oil in a screw-top jar and shake. Turn out the loaf, cut into slices and serve with the dressing.

NUTRITION PER SERVE
Protein 7.8 g; Fat 8.4 g; Carbohydrate 42.8 g; Dietary Fibre 3.7 g; Cholesterol 6 mg; 1202 kJ (287 Cal)

Cook the tomatoes, zucchini and corn over high heat until soft.

Mix together the onion mixture, vegetables, capsicum, basil and couscous.

Lentil rissoles

PREPARATION TIME: 20 MINUTES + 40 MINUTES COOLING | TOTAL COOKING TIME: 45 MINUTES | SERVES 4

1 tablespoon oil
1 onion, finely chopped
2 large garlic cloves, crushed
2 teaspoons ground cumin
1 teaspoon ground coriander
1 small carrot, finely diced
250 g (9 oz/1 cup) red lentils
120 g (4 oz/1½ cups) fresh wholemeal (whole-wheat) breadcrumbs
60 g (2¼ oz/⅔ cup) walnuts, finely chopped
90 g (3¼ oz/½ cup) frozen peas
3 tablespoons chopped flat-leaf (Italian) parsley
dry breadcrumbs, for coating
oil, for shallow-frying

1 Heat the oil in a large saucepan. Cook the onion, garlic, cumin and ground coriander over medium heat for 2 minutes, or until the onion has softened. Stir in the carrot, lentils and 500 ml (17 fl oz/2 cups) water. Slowly bring to the boil, then reduce the heat to low and simmer, covered, for 25–30 minutes, or until the lentils are cooked and pulpy, stirring frequently to stop them sticking and burning. Remove the lid during the last 10 minutes to evaporate any remaining liquid.

2 Transfer the mixture to a large bowl, cover with plastic wrap and cool for 10 minutes. Stir in the fresh breadcrumbs, walnuts, peas and parsley. Form into eight 8 cm (3¼ inch) round rissoles. Cover and refrigerate for 30 minutes, or until they are firm.

3 Evenly coat the rissoles in dry breadcrumbs, shaking off any excess. Heat 1 cm (½ inch) oil in a deep frying pan, add the rissoles and cook in two batches for 3 minutes on each side, or until golden brown. Drain on crumpled paper towels, season with salt and serve with a salad.

Cover the pan and simmer the lentils until they are cooked and pulpy.

With clean hands, form the mixture into eight round rissoles.

NUTRITION PER SERVE
Protein 24 g; Fat 20 g; Carbohydrate 50 g; Dietary Fibre 14 g; Cholesterol 0 mg; 2014 kJ (480 Cal)

Carrot and pumpkin risotto

PREPARATION TIME: 15 MINUTES | TOTAL COOKING TIME: 35 MINUTES | SERVES 4

90 g (3¼ oz) butter
1 onion, finely chopped
250 g (9 oz) pumpkin (winter squash), diced
2 carrots, diced
2 litres (70 fl oz/8 cups) vegetable stock
440 g (15½ oz/2 cups) arborio rice
90 g (3¼ oz) romano cheese, grated (see NOTE)
¼ teaspoon nutmeg

1 Heat 60 g (2 oz) of the butter in a large, heavy-based saucepan. Add the onion and fry for 1–2 minutes, or until soft. Add the pumpkin and carrot and cook for 6–8 minutes, or until tender. Mash slightly with a potato masher. In a separate saucepan keep the stock at simmering point.

2 Add the rice to the vegetables and cook for 1 minute, stirring constantly until the grains are translucent. Ladle in 125 ml (4 fl oz/½ cup) hot stock and stir well. Reduce the heat and add the stock little by little, stirring constantly for 20–25 minutes, or until the rice is tender and creamy. (You may not need to add all the stock, or you may run out and need to use a little water. Every risotto is different.)

3 Remove from the heat, add the remaining butter, cheese, nutmeg and freshly ground black pepper and fork through. Cover and leave for 5 minutes before serving.

NOTE: *Romano is a hard, Italian grating cheese similar to parmesan. Parmesan is a good substitute.*

NUTRITION PER SERVE
Protein 27 g; Fat 34 g; Carbohydrate 95 g; Dietary Fibre 5 g; Cholesterol 100 mg; 3318 kJ (793 Cal)

Cook the pumpkin and carrot until tender, then mash a little.

The secret to good risotto is to add the stock a little at a time and stir constantly.

Silverbeet parcels

PREPARATION TIME: 40 MINUTES | TOTAL COOKING TIME: 1 HOUR | SERVES 6

500 ml (17 fl oz/2 cups) vegetable stock
1 tablespoon olive oil
1 onion, chopped
2 garlic cloves, crushed
1 red capsicum (pepper), chopped
250 g (9 oz) mushrooms, chopped
110 g (3¾ oz/½ cup) arborio rice
60 g (2¼ oz) cheddar cheese, grated
2 small handfuls shredded basil
6 large silverbeet leaves
2 x 400 g (14 oz) tins chopped tomatoes
1 tablespoon balsamic vinegar
1 teaspoon soft brown sugar

NUTRITION PER SERVE
Protein 7.5 g; Fat 6 g; Carbohydrate 20 g; Dietary Fibre 4 g; Cholesterol 7 mg; 725 kJ (175 Cal)

1 Heat the vegetable stock in a saucepan and maintain at simmering point. Heat the oil in a large saucepan, add the onion and garlic and cook until the onion has softened. Add the capsicum, mushrooms and rice and stir until well combined. Gradually add 125 ml (4 fl oz/½ cup) hot stock, stirring until the liquid has been absorbed. Continue to add the stock, a little at a time, stirring constantly for 20–25 minutes, or until the rice is creamy and tender (you may not need all the stock, or you may need to add a little water if you run out). Remove from the heat, add the cheese and basil and season well.

2 Trim the stalks from the silverbeet and cook the leaves, a few at a time, in a large saucepan of boiling water for 30 seconds, or until wilted. Drain on a tea towel (dish towel). Using a sharp knife, cut away any tough white veins from the centre of the leaves without cutting them in half. If necessary, overlap the two sides to make a flat surface. Place a portion of the filling in the centre of each leaf, fold in the sides and roll up carefully. Tie with string.

3 Put the tomato, balsamic vinegar and sugar in a large, deep non-stick frying pan and stir to combine. Add the silverbeet parcels, cover and simmer for 10 minutes. Remove the string and serve with the tomato sauce.

Add the stock, a little at a time, until the rice is tender and has absorbed the stock.

Using a sharp knife, cut away the white veins from the centre of the leaves.

Place the filling in the centre of each leaf, fold in the sides and roll up into parcels.

Grilled polenta with wild mushrooms

PREPARATION TIME: 30 MINUTES + 2 HOURS CHILLING | TOTAL COOKING TIME: 1 HOUR 20 MINUTES | SERVES 6–8

600 ml (21 fl oz/2½ cups) vegetable stock
300 g (10½ oz/2 cups) polenta
100 g (3½ oz) parmesan cheese, grated

MUSHROOM SAUCE
1 kg (2 lb 4 oz) mixed mushrooms (roman, oyster and flat)
125 ml (4 fl oz/½ cup) olive oil
1 large handful chopped parsley
4 garlic cloves, finely chopped
1 onion, chopped

1 Put the stock and 500 ml (17 fl oz/2 cups) water in a large saucepan and bring to the boil. Add the polenta and stir constantly for 10 minutes until very thick. Remove from the heat and stir in the parmesan. Brush a 20 cm (8 inch) round spring-form cake tin with oil. Spread the polenta into the tin and smooth the surface. Refrigerate for 2 hours, turn out and cut into quarters, then quarter each wedge (so you will end up with 16 slices).

2 To make the sauce, wipe the mushrooms with a damp cloth and roughly chop the larger ones. Put the mushrooms, oil, parsley, garlic and onion in a saucepan. Stir, cover and leave to simmer for 50 minutes, or until cooked through. Uncover and cook for 10 minutes, or until there is very little liquid left. Set aside.

3 Brush one side of the polenta with olive oil and cook under a preheated grill (broiler) for 5 minutes, or until the edges are browned. Turn over and brown. Reheat the mushroom sauce and serve the slices of polenta over the sauce.

NOTE: *Use just button mushrooms if the other varieties aren't available.*

Stir the polenta until very thick, remove from the heat and add the parmesan.

Refrigerate the tin of polenta for 2 hours, then turn out and cut into wedges.

NUTRITION PER SERVE (6)
Protein 11 g; Fat 20 g; Carbohydrate 11 g; Dietary Fibre 4 g; Cholesterol 12 mg; 1103 kJ (214 Cal)

Red lentil pilau

PREPARATION TIME: 15 MINUTES | TOTAL COOKING TIME: 25 MINUTES | SERVES 4–6

GARAM MASALA
1 tablespoon coriander seeds
1 tablespoon cardamom pods
1 tablespoon cumin seeds
1 teaspoon whole black peppercorns
1 teaspoon whole cloves
1 small cinnamon stick, crushed

3 tablespoons oil
1 onion, chopped
3 garlic cloves, chopped
200 g (7 oz/1 cup) basmati rice
250 g (9 oz/1 cup) red lentils
750 ml (26 fl oz/3 cups) hot vegetable stock
spring onions (scallions), shredded to serve

1 To make the garam masala, place all the spices in a dry frying pan and shake over medium heat for 1 minute, or until fragrant. Blend in a spice grinder, blender or mortar and pestle to make a fine powder.

2 Heat the oil in a large saucepan. Add the onion, garlic and 3 teaspoons of garam masala. Cook over medium heat for 3 minutes, or until soft.

3 Stir in the rice and lentils and cook for 2 minutes. Add the hot stock and stir well. Slowly bring to the boil, then reduce the heat and simmer, covered, for 15–20 minutes, or until the rice is cooked and all the stock has been absorbed. Gently fluff the rice with a fork. Garnish with the spring onion.

NOTE: *If time is short you can use ready-made garam masala instead of making your own.*

Finely blend all the spices in a spice grinder until they make a fine powder.

Stir the rice and lentils into the onion and garlic mixture and cook for 2 minutes.

NUTRITION PER SERVE (6)
Protein 13 g; Fat 11 g; Carbohydrate 42 g; Dietary Fibre 7 g; Cholesterol 0 mg; 1333 kJ (318 Cal)

Tofu with carrot and ginger sauce

PREPARATION TIME: 25 MINUTES + OVERNIGHT MARINATING | TOTAL COOKING TIME: 30 MINUTES | SERVES 6

2 x 300 g (10½ oz) packets firm tofu
125 ml (4 fl oz/½ cup) freshly squeezed orange juice
1 tablespoon soft brown sugar
1 tablespoon soy sauce
2 tablespoons chopped coriander (cilantro) leaves
2 garlic cloves, crushed
1 teaspoon grated fresh ginger
2–3 tablespoons oil
1 kg (2 lb 4 oz) baby bok choy (pak choy), cut into quarters lengthways

CARROT AND GINGER SAUCE

300 g (10½ oz) carrots, chopped
2 teaspoons grated fresh ginger
170 ml (5½ fl oz/⅔ cup) orange juice
125 ml (4 fl oz/½ cup) vegetable stock

NUTRITION PER SERVE
Protein 14 g; Fat 14 g; Carbohydrate 14 g; Dietary Fibre 8.5 g; Cholesterol 0 mg; 1034 kJ (246 Cal)

1 Drain the tofu, then slice each block into six lengthways. Place in a single layer in a flat non-metallic dish. Mix the juice, sugar, soy sauce, coriander, garlic and ginger in a bowl, then pour over the tofu. Cover and refrigerate overnight, turning once.

2 Drain the tofu, reserving the marinade. Heat the oil in a large frying pan and cook the tofu in batches over high heat for 2–3 minutes on each side, or until golden. Remove and keep warm. Bring the marinade to the boil in a saucepan, then reduce the heat and simmer for 1 minute. Remove from the heat and keep warm.

3 Heat a wok, add the bok choy and 1 tablespoon water and cook, covered, over medium heat for 2–3 minutes, or until tender. Remove and keep warm.

4 Put all the sauce ingredients in a saucepan, bring to the boil, then reduce the heat and simmer, covered, for 5–6 minutes, or until the carrot is tender. Transfer to a food processor and blend until smooth.

5 To serve, divide the carrot and ginger sauce and bok choy among six plates. Top with the tofu and drizzle on a little of the marinade before serving.

Use a non-metallic dish for marinating in acidic liquids such as orange juice.

Cook the tofu slices in batches until golden brown on both sides.

Blend the carrot and ginger sauce in a food processor until smooth.

Chickpea patties with caramelised onion

PREPARATION TIME: 20 MINUTES | TOTAL COOKING TIME: 30 MINUTES | SERVES 4

1 tablespoon olive oil
1 red onion, finely chopped
2 garlic cloves, crushed
1 tablespoon ground cumin
2 x 310 g (11 oz) tins chickpeas, drained and rinsed
30 g (1 oz/¼ cup) sunflower seeds
1 very large handful finely chopped coriander (cilantro) leaves
2 eggs, lightly beaten
75 g (2½ oz/⅔ cup) besan (chickpea) flour
oil, for shallow-frying
rocket (arugula) leaves, to serve

CARAMELISED ONION

40 g (1½ oz) butter
2 red onions, thinly sliced
3 teaspoons soft brown sugar
plain yoghurt, to serve

1 Heat the oil in a frying pan, add the onion and cook over medium heat for 3 minutes, or until soft. Add the garlic and cumin and cook for 1 minute. Allow to cool slightly.

2 Blend the chickpeas, sunflower seeds, coriander, egg and onion mixture in a food processor until smooth. Fold in the besan flour and season. Divide the mixture into eight portions and, using floured hands, form into patties. Heat 1 cm (½ inch) of oil in a frying pan and cook the patties in two batches over medium heat for 2–3 minutes on each side, or until firm. Drain on paper towels. Keep warm.

3 To make the caramelised onion, melt the butter in a small frying pan and cook the onion over medium heat for 10 minutes, stirring occasionally. Add the sugar and cook for 1 minute, or until caramelised. Serve with yoghurt and rocket on the side.

Shallow-fry the chickpea patties in batches, until firm and golden on both sides.

Cook the onion for 10 minutes, then stir in the sugar and cook until caramelised.

NUTRITION PER SERVE
Protein 35 g; Fat 38 g; Carbohydrate 70 g; Dietary Fibre 23 g; Cholesterol 116 mg; 3170 kJ (757 Cal)

Asparagus and pistachio risotto

PREPARATION TIME: 10 MINUTES | TOTAL COOKING TIME: 30 MINUTES | SERVES 4–6

1 litre (35 fl oz/4 cups) vegetable stock
250 ml (9 fl oz/1 cup) dry white wine
4 tablespoons extra virgin olive oil
1 red onion, finely chopped
440 g (15½ oz/2 cups) arborio rice
310 g (11 oz) asparagus spears, trimmed and cut into short lengths
125 ml (4 fl oz/½ cup) pouring (whipping) cream
100 g (3½ oz/1 cup) grated parmesan cheese
40 g (1½ oz/½ cup) shelled pistachio nuts, toasted and roughly chopped

1 Heat the stock and wine in a large saucepan and keep at simmering point on the stove top.

2 Heat the oil in another large saucepan. Add the onion and cook over medium heat for 3 minutes, or until soft. Add the rice and stir for 1 minute, or until translucent.

3 Add 125 ml (4 fl oz/½ cup) hot stock, stirring constantly until the liquid is absorbed. Continue adding more stock, a little at a time, stirring constantly for 20–25 minutes, or until the rice is tender and creamy (you may not need to add all the stock, or you may not have quite enough and will need to add a little water as well—every risotto is different). Add the asparagus during the last 5 minutes of cooking.

4 Remove from the heat and leave for 2 minutes, then stir in the cream and parmesan and season well. Serve sprinkled with pistachios.

Add the rice to the saucepan and stir until the grains are translucent.

Leave the risotto to stand for 2 minutes, then stir in the cream and parmesan.

NUTRITION PER SERVE (6)
Protein 15 g; Fat 30 g; Carbohydrate 60 g; Dietary Fibre 3.5 g; Cholesterol 45 mg; 2425 kJ (580 Cal)

Asian barley pilau

PREPARATION TIME: 10 MINUTES + 15 MINUTES STANDING | TOTAL COOKING TIME: 35 MINUTES | SERVES 4

15 g (½ oz) dried sliced button mushrooms
500 ml (17 fl oz/2 cups) vegetable stock
125 ml (4 fl oz/½ cup) dry sherry
1 tablespoon oil
3 large French shallots (eschalots), thinly sliced
2 large garlic cloves, crushed
1 tablespoon grated fresh ginger
1 teaspoon sichuan peppercorns, crushed (see NOTE)
330 g (11½ oz/1½ cups) pearl barley
500 g (1 lb 2 oz) choy sum (Chinese flowering cabbage), cut into short lengths
3 teaspoons kecap manis (see NOTE, page 42)
1 teaspoon sesame oil

NUTRITION PER SERVE
Protein 13 g; Fat 8.5 g; Carbohydrate 52 g; Dietary Fibre 13 g; Cholesterol 0 mg; 1552 kJ (370 Cal)

1 Place the mushrooms in a bowl and cover with boiling water, then leave for 15 minutes. Strain carefully, reserving 125 ml (4 fl oz/ ½ cup) of the liquid.

2 Bring the stock and sherry to the boil in a saucepan, then reduce the heat, cover and simmer until needed.

3 Heat the oil in a large saucepan and cook the shallots over medium heat for 2–3 minutes, or until soft. Add the garlic, ginger and peppercorns and cook for 1 minute. Add the barley and mushrooms and mix well. Stir in the stock and mushroom liquid, then reduce the heat and simmer, covered, for 25 minutes, or until the liquid evaporates.

4 Meanwhile, steam the choy sum until wilted. Add to the barley mixture. Stir in the kecap manis and sesame oil to serve.

NOTE: *You can buy sichuan peppercorns at Asian food stores.*

French shallots are like small onions. Peel them and then slice thinly.

Strain the mushrooms, reserving some of the liquid for flavouring the pilau.

Reduce the heat and simmer the pilau until the liquid has evaporated.

Couscous patties

PREPARATION TIME: 35 MINUTES + 15 MINUTES REFRIGERATION + 10 MINUTES STANDING | TOTAL COOKING TIME: 30 MINUTES | MAKES 4

185 g (6½ oz/1 cup) couscous
4 tablespoons oil
1 eggplant (aubergine), finely diced
1 onion, finely chopped
1 garlic clove, crushed
2 teaspoons ground cumin
2 teaspoons ground coriander
1 red capsicum (pepper), finely diced
2 tablespoons chopped coriander (cilantro)
2 teaspoons grated lemon zest
2 teaspoons lemon juice
5 tablespoons plain yoghurt
1 egg, lightly beaten
oil, for shallow-frying

1 Place the couscous in a bowl. Add 250 ml (9 fl oz/1 cup) of boiling water and leave for 10 minutes, or until all the water has been absorbed. Fluff up the grains with a fork.

2 Heat 2 tablespoons of the oil in a large frying pan and fry the eggplant until soft and golden, then place in a bowl. Heat 1 tablespoon of the oil in the pan. Add the onion, garlic, cumin and ground coriander. Cook over medium heat for 3–4 minutes, or until soft, then add to the bowl. Heat the remaining oil and cook the capsicum for 5 minutes, or until soft. Place in the bowl and stir well.

3 Add the vegetable mixture to the couscous with the fresh coriander, lemon zest, lemon juice, yoghurt and egg. Season to taste and mix well. Using damp hands, divide the mixture into four portions and form into large patties—they should be about 2 cm (¾ inch) thick. Cover and refrigerate for 15 minutes. Shallow-fry the patties over medium heat for 5 minutes on each side, or until golden. Drain the patties well and serve with semi-dried tomatoes and spinach on the side, if desired.

When the couscous has absorbed the water, fluff up the grains with a fork.

With damp hands, gently form the mixture into four large patties.

NUTRITION PER PATTY
Protein 9 g; Fat 25 g; Carbohydrate 35 g; Dietary Fibre 4 g; Cholesterol 5 mg; 1760 kJ (420 Cal)

Caraway polenta with braised leeks

PREPARATION TIME: 10 MINUTES | TOTAL COOKING TIME: 30 MINUTES | SERVES 4

1.5 litres (52 fl oz/6 cups) vegetable stock
225 g (8 oz/1½ cups) polenta
2 teaspoons caraway seeds
45 g (1½ oz) butter
2 large leeks, white part only, cut into thin strips
250 g (9 oz) fontina cheese, cubed

1 Place the stock in a large heavy-based saucepan and bring to the boil. Pour in the polenta in a fine stream, stirring continuously. Add the caraway seeds and then reduce the heat and simmer for about 20–25 minutes, or until the polenta is very soft.

2 Melt the butter in a frying pan over medium heat and add the leeks. Cover and cook gently, stirring often, until wilted. Add the fontina, stir a couple of times and remove from the heat.

3 Pour the polenta onto plates in nest shapes and spoon the leeks and cheese into the centre.

HINT: *Ready-made stock can be quite salty, so use half stock, half water.*

NOTE: *Polenta is also known as cornmeal and is available from most supermarkets and delicatessens.*

NUTRITION PER SERVE
Protein 17 g; Fat 25 g; Carbohydrate 40 g; Dietary Fibre 3 g; Cholesterol 72 mg; 1908 kJ (456 Cal)

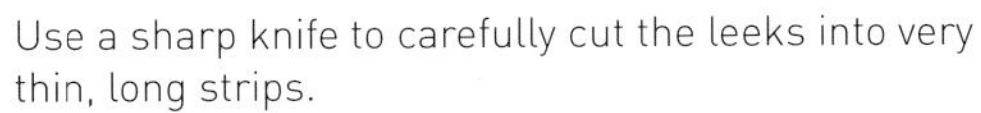

Use a sharp knife to carefully cut the leeks into very thin, long strips.

Bring the stock to the boil, then pour in the polenta, stirring continuously.

Cook the leeks in the butter until wilted, then stir in the cheese.

Miso tofu sticks with cucumber and wakame salad

PREPARATION TIME: 30 MINUTES + 20 MINUTES STANDING | TOTAL COOKING TIME: 15 MINUTES | SERVES 4

3 Lebanese (short) cucumbers, thinly sliced
20 g (¾ oz) dried wakame
500 g (1 lb 2 oz) silken firm tofu, well drained
3 tablespoons shiro miso (see NOTE)
1 tablespoon mirin
1 tablespoon sugar
1 tablespoon rice vinegar
1 egg yolk
100 g (3½ oz) bean sprouts, trimmed and blanched

DRESSING
3 tablespoons rice vinegar
¼ teaspoon soy sauce
1½ tablespoons sugar
1 tablespoon mirin

NUTRITION PER SERVE
Protein 10 g; Fat 7 g; Carbohydrate 8 g; Dietary Fibre 2.5 g; Cholesterol 0 mg; 710 kJ (180 Cal)

1 Sprinkle the cucumber generously with salt and leave for 20 minutes, or until very soft, then rinse and drain. To rehydrate the wakame, place it in a colander in the sink and leave it under cold running water for 10 minutes, then drain well.

2 Place the tofu in a colander, weigh down with a plate and leave to drain.

3 Place the shiro miso, mirin, sugar, rice vinegar and 2 tablespoons water in a saucepan and stir over low heat for 1 minute, or until the sugar dissolves. Remove from the heat, then add the egg yolk and whisk until glossy. Cool slightly.

4 Cut the tofu into thick sticks and place on a non-stick baking tray. Brush the miso mixture over the tofu and cook under a hot grill (broiler) for 6 minutes on each side, or until light golden on both sides.

5 To make the dressing, place all the ingredients and ½ teaspoon of salt in a bowl and whisk together well.

6 To assemble, place the cucumber in the centre of a plate, top with the sprouts and wakame, drizzle with the dressing, top with tofu and serve topped with some more sprouts.

NOTE: *Shiro miso is a white miso. It is available from Asian stores.*

Once the cucumber is very soft, rinse the salt off under running water.

Place the wakame in a colander and leave it under cold running water.

Brush the miso mixture over the tofu sticks and grill until golden.

Mushroom risotto

PREPARATION TIME: 15 MINUTES | TOTAL COOKING TIME: 40 MINUTES | SERVES 4

1.5 litres (52 fl oz/6 cups) vegetable stock
500 ml (17 fl oz/2 cups) dry white wine
2 tablespoons olive oil
60 g (2¼ oz) butter
2 leeks, thinly sliced
1 kg (2 lb 4 oz) field mushrooms, sliced
500 g (1 lb 2 oz) arborio rice
75 g (2½ oz/¾ cup) grated parmesan cheese, plus shavings, to serve
3 tablespoons chopped flat-leaf (Italian) parsley
balsamic vinegar, to serve

1 Place the stock and wine in a large saucepan and keep at simmering point on the stove top.

2 Heat the oil and butter in a large saucepan. Add the leek and cook over medium heat for 5 minutes, or until soft and golden. Add the mushrooms to the pan and cook for 5 minutes, or until tender. Add the rice and stir for 1 minute, or until translucent.

3 Add 125 ml (4 fl oz/½ cup) hot stock, stirring constantly over medium heat until the liquid is absorbed. Continue adding the stock, a little at a time, stirring constantly for 20–25 minutes, or until all the rice is tender and creamy (you may not need to add all the stock, or you may not have quite enough and will need to add a little water as well—every risotto is different).

4 Stir in the parmesan and chopped parsley and heat for 1 minute, or until all the cheese has melted. Serve drizzled with balsamic vinegar and topped with parmesan shavings.

Stir the rice constantly until most of the liquid has been absorbed.

Once the rice is tender, stir the grated parmesan and parsley into the risotto.

NUTRITION PER SERVE
Protein 26 g; Fat 30 g; Carbohydrate 105 g; Dietary Fibre 11 g; Cholesterol 56 mg; 3299 kJ (788 Cal)

Barbecue vegetable and tofu kebabs

PREPARATION TIME: 40 MINUTES + 30 MINUTES MARINATING | TOTAL COOKING TIME: 30 MINUTES | SERVES 4

500 g (1 lb 2 oz) firm tofu, cubed
1 red capsicum (pepper), cut into squares
3 zucchini (courgettes), thickly sliced
4 small onions, cut into quarters
300 g (10½ oz) button mushrooms, quartered
125 ml (4 fl oz/½ cup) tamari
125 ml (4 fl oz/½ cup) sesame oil
2.5 cm (1 inch) piece fresh ginger, peeled and grated
175 g (6 oz/½ cup) honey

PEANUT SAUCE
1 tablespoon sesame oil
1 small onion, finely chopped
1 garlic clove, crushed
2 teaspoons chilli paste
250 g (9 oz/1 cup) smooth peanut butter
250 ml (9 fl oz/1 cup) coconut milk
1 tablespoon soft brown sugar
1 tablespoon tamari
1 tablespoon lemon juice
40 g (1½ oz/¼ cup) peanuts, roasted, chopped
40 g (1½ oz/¼ cup) sesame seeds, toasted

1 Soak 12 bamboo skewers in water for 2 hours. Alternate tofu, capsicum, zucchini, onions and mushrooms onto the skewers.

2 Combine tamari, oil, ginger and honey in a non-metallic bowl. Pour over the kebabs. Leave for 30 minutes. Cook in a chargrill pan, turning, for 10–15 minutes. Remove and keep warm. For peanut sauce, heat oil in a frying pan over medium heat and cook onion, garlic and chilli paste for 1–2 minutes. Reduce heat, add peanut butter, coconut milk, sugar, tamari and lemon juice. Stir. Bring to the boil. Reduce heat and simmer for 10 minutes, or until thick. Stir in the peanuts. If the sauce is too thick, add water. Serve with kebabs, sprinkled with sesame seeds.

NUTRITION PER SERVE
Protein 31.5 g; Fat 65 g; Carbohydrate 25.5 g; Dietary Fibre 15 g; Cholesterol 0 mg; 3334 kJ (795 Cal)

Thread alternating pieces of tofu and vegetables onto the skewers.

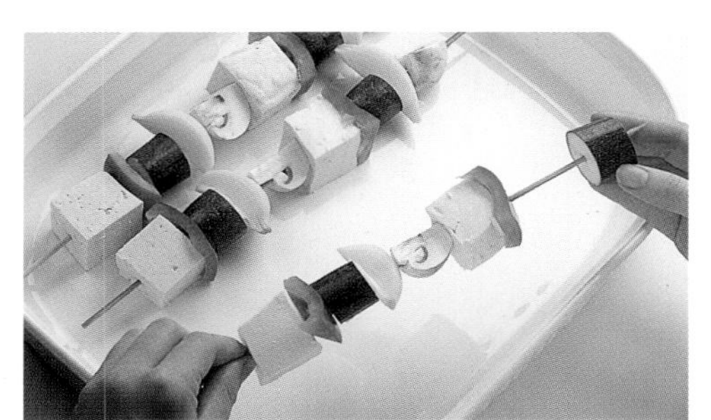

Cook the skewers on a barbecue grill plate or flat plate, occasionally turning and basting them.

Baked polenta with four cheeses

PREPARATION TIME: 20 MINUTES + 2 HOURS CHILLING | TOTAL COOKING TIME: 45 MINUTES | SERVES 4

POLENTA
625 ml (21½ fl oz/2½ cups) vegetable stock
300 g (10½ oz/2 cups) polenta (see NOTE)
60 g (2¼ oz/½ cup) grated parmesan cheese

CHEESE FILLING
100 g (3½ oz) havarti cheese, sliced
100 g (3½ oz) mascarpone cheese
100 g (3½ oz) blue cheese, crumbled
100 g (3½ oz) butter, sliced thinly
60 g (2¼ oz/½ cup) grated parmesan cheese

NUTRITION PER SERVE
Protein 20 g; Fat 38 g; Carbohydrate 35 g; Dietary Fibre 1.5 g; Cholesterol 113 mg; 2351 kJ (560 Cal)

1 To make the polenta, brush a 1.75 litre (60 fl oz/7 cup) loaf tin with oil. Put the stock and 500 ml (17 fl oz/2 cups) water in a large pan and bring to the boil. Add the polenta and stir for 10 minutes until very thick.

2 Remove from the heat and stir in the parmesan. Spread into the tin and smooth the surface. Refrigerate for 2 hours, then cut into about 30 thin slices. Preheat the oven to 180°C (350°F/Gas 4).

3 Brush a large ovenproof dish with oil. Place a layer of polenta slices on the base. Top with a layer of half the combined havarti, mascarpone and blue cheeses and half the butter. Add another layer of polenta and top with the remainder of the three cheeses and butter. Add a final layer of polenta and sprinkle the parmesan on top. Bake for 30 minutes, or until a golden crust forms. Serve immediately.

NOTE: *Polenta is also known as cornmeal and is available from most supermarkets and delicatessens.*

Havarti is a Danish cheese with a full flavour.

Add the polenta to the stock and water and stir constantly until very thick.

Use the back of a spoon to spread the polenta in the tin.

Build up the layers of sliced polenta, butter and different cheeses.

Casseroles, curries and bakes

Mushroom moussaka

PREPARATION TIME: 20 MINUTES | TOTAL COOKING TIME: 1 HOUR | SERVES 4–6

- 1 eggplant (aubergine), cut into 1 cm (½ inch) slices
- 1 large potato, cut into 1 cm (½ inch) slices
- 30 g (1 oz) butter
- 1 onion, finely chopped
- 2 garlic cloves, finely chopped
- 500 g (1 lb 2 oz) flat mushrooms, sliced
- 400 g (14 oz) tin chopped tomatoes
- ½ teaspoon sugar
- 40 g (1½ oz) butter, extra
- 40 g (1½ oz/⅓ cup) plain (all-purpose) flour
- 500 ml (17 fl oz/2 cups) milk
- 1 egg, lightly beaten
- 40 g (1½ oz) grated parmesan cheese

NUTRITION PER SERVE (6)
Protein 12 g; Fat 16 g; Carbohydrate 18 g; Dietary Fibre 5 g; Cholesterol 77 mg; 1125 kJ (268 Cal)

1 Preheat the oven to 220°C (425°F/Gas 7). Line a large baking tray with foil and brush with oil. Put the eggplant and potato in a single layer on the tray and sprinkle with salt and pepper. Bake for 20 minutes.

2 Melt the butter in a large frying pan over medium heat. Add the onion and cook, stirring, for 3–4 minutes, or until soft. Add the garlic and cook for 1 minute, or until fragrant. Increase the heat to high, add the mushrooms and stir continuously for 2–3 minutes, or until soft. Add the tomato, reduce the heat and simmer rapidly for 8 minutes, or until reduced. Stir in the sugar.

3 Melt the extra butter in a large saucepan over low heat. Add the flour and cook for 1 minute, or until pale and foaming. Remove from the heat and gradually stir in the milk. Return to the heat and stir constantly until it boils and thickens. Reduce the heat and simmer for 2 minutes. Remove from the heat and, when the bubbles subside, stir in the egg and parmesan.

4 Reduce the oven to 180°C (350°F/Gas 4). Grease a shallow 1.5 litre (52 fl oz/6 cup) ovenproof dish. Spoon one-third of the mushroom mixture into the dish. Cover with potato and top with half the remaining mushrooms, then the eggplant. Finish with the remaining mushrooms, pour on the sauce and smooth the top. Bake for 30–35 minutes, or until the edges bubble. Leave for 10 minutes before serving.

A small amount of sugar added to the tomato mixture will bring out the flavours.

Remove the saucepan from the heat and stir in the egg and parmesan.

Cover the tomato and mushroom mixture with the potato slices.

Green curry with sweet potato and eggplant

PREPARATION TIME: 15 MINUTES | TOTAL COOKING TIME: 25 MINUTES | SERVES 4–6

1 tablespoon oil
1 onion, chopped
1–2 tablespoons green curry paste (see NOTE)
1 eggplant (aubergine), quartered and sliced
375 ml (13 fl oz/1½ cups) coconut milk
250 ml (9 fl oz/1 cup) vegetable stock
6 makrut (kaffir lime) leaves
1 orange sweet potato, cubed
2 teaspoons soft brown sugar
2 tablespoons lime juice
2 teaspoons lime zest

1 Heat the oil in a large wok or frying pan. Add the onion and green curry paste and cook, stirring, over medium heat for 3 minutes. Add the eggplant and cook for a further 4–5 minutes, or until softened.

2 Pour in the coconut milk and vegetable stock, bring to the boil, then reduce the heat and simmer for 5 minutes. Add the makrut leaves and sweet potato and cook for 10 minutes, or until the eggplant and sweet potato are very tender.

3 Mix in the sugar, lime juice and zest until well combined with the vegetables. Season to taste with salt and serve with steamed rice.

NOTE: *Strict vegetarians should be sure to read the label and choose a green curry paste that doesn't contain shrimp paste. Alternatively, make your own curry pastes.*

Use a sharp knife to quarter and slice the eggplant.

Cook, stirring occasionally, until the vegetables are very tender.

NUTRITION PER SERVE (6)
Protein 2.5 g; Fat 17 g; Carbohydrate 10 g; Dietary Fibre 3 g; Cholesterol 0.5 mg; 835 kJ (200 Cal)

Bean and capsicum stew

PREPARATION TIME: 20 MINUTES + OVERNIGHT SOAKING | TOTAL COOKING TIME: 1 HOUR 35 MINUTES | SERVES 4–6

200 g (7 oz/1 cup) dried haricot beans (see NOTE)
2 tablespoons olive oil
2 large garlic cloves, crushed
1 red onion, halved and cut into thin wedges
1 red capsicum (pepper), cut into squares
1 green capsicum (pepper), cut into squares
2 x 400 g (14 oz) tins chopped tomatoes
2 tablespoons tomato paste (concentrated purée)
500 ml (17 fl oz/2 cups) vegetable stock
2 tablespoons chopped basil
125 g (4½ oz/⅔ cup) kalamata olives, pitted
1–2 teaspoons soft brown sugar

1 Put the beans in a large bowl, cover with cold water and soak overnight. Rinse well, then transfer to a saucepan, cover with cold water and cook for 45 minutes, or until just tender. Drain.

2 Heat the oil in a large saucepan. Cook the garlic and onion over medium heat for 2–3 minutes, or until the onion is soft. Add the red and green capsicums and cook for a further 5 minutes.

3 Stir in the tomato, tomato paste, stock and beans. Simmer, covered, for 40 minutes, or until the beans are cooked through. Stir in the basil, olives and sugar. Season with salt and freshly ground black pepper. Serve hot with crusty bread.

NOTE: *1 cup of dried haricot beans yields about 2½ cups cooked beans. So use 2½ cups tinned haricot or borlotti beans instead, if you prefer.*

NUTRITION PER SERVE (6)
Protein 10 g; Fat 8 g; Carbohydrate 20 g; Dietary Fibre 9.5 g; Cholesterol 0 mg; 825 kJ (197 Cal)

Cook the garlic and onion until the garlic is soft, then add the capsicum.

Simmer the stew for 40 minutes, or until the beans are cooked through.

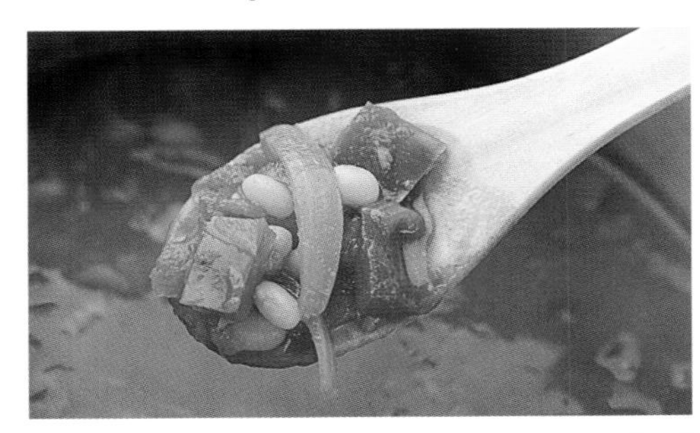

Cheese and spinach pancakes

PREPARATION TIME: 40 MINUTES | TOTAL COOKING TIME: 50 MINUTES | SERVES 4

250 g (9 oz) cooked, drained English spinach, chopped
125 g (4½ oz/½ cup) ricotta cheese
30 g (1 oz/¼ cup) grated cheddar cheese
freshly grated nutmeg
25 g (1 oz/¼ cup) grated parmesan cheese
½ teaspoon paprika
40 g (1½ oz/½ cup) fresh breadcrumbs

BATTER
125 g (4½ oz/1 cup) plain (all-purpose) flour
310 ml (10¾ fl oz/1¼ cups) milk
1 egg
butter, for cooking

CHEESE SAUCE
2 tablespoons butter
30 g (1 oz/¼ cup) plain (all-purpose) flour
435 ml (15¼ fl oz/1¾ cups) milk
125 g (4½ oz/1 cup) grated cheddar cheese

1 Put the spinach, ricotta, cheddar and nutmeg in a bowl and mix well.

2 To make batter, sift the flour and a pinch of salt into a bowl. Add half the milk and the egg. Whisk until smooth; add the remaining milk. Heat a teaspoon of butter in a frying pan and pour in a thin layer of batter. Cook the base until golden, then flip. The batter should make 8 pancakes.

3 To make the cheese sauce, melt the butter over low heat, stir in the flour until smooth and cook for 1 minute. Remove from the heat and slowly stir in the milk. Bring to the boil, stirring constantly. Remove from the heat and add salt and freshly ground black pepper and the grated cheddar.

4 Preheat the oven to 180°C (350°F/ Gas 4). Divide the filling among the pancakes, roll up and put in a greased ovenproof dish. Pour the cheese sauce over the pancakes. Mix the parmesan, paprika and breadcrumbs together and sprinkle over the sauce. Bake for 30 minutes, or until golden brown.

NUTRITION PER SERVE
Protein 18 g; Fat 17 g; Carbohydrate 34 g; Dietary Fibre 3 g; Cholesterol 96 mg; 1511 kJ (360 Cal)

Put the spinach, cheese, pepper and nutmeg in a bowl and mix well.

Cook until both sides of the pancake are golden, then remove with a spatula.

Divide the filling among the pancakes, roll up and put in the greased ovenproof dish.

Stuffed zucchini

PREPARATION TIME: 20 MINUTES | TOTAL COOKING TIME: 45 MINUTES | SERVES 4

- 8 zucchini (courgettes)
- 35 g (1¼ oz) white bread, crusts removed
- milk, for soaking
- 125 g (4½ oz) ricotta cheese
- 3 tablespoons grated cheddar cheese
- 35 g (1¼ oz/⅓ cup) grated parmesan cheese
- 2 teaspoons chopped oregano, plus extra sprigs, to garnish
- 2 teaspoons chopped thyme
- 1 garlic clove, crushed
- 1 egg yolk

1 Preheat the oven to 190°C (375°F/Gas 5). Cook the zucchini in boiling salted water for 5 minutes, then drain. Meanwhile, soak the bread in milk until soft, then squeeze dry. Cut the zucchini in half and scoop out the flesh with a teaspoon. Chop the zucchini flesh finely. Place in a bowl and add the bread, cheeses, herbs, garlic, egg yolk and season with salt and freshly ground black pepper. Mix together, adding a little milk to make it bind if necessary.

2 Fill the zucchini shells with the stuffing. Brush an ovenproof baking dish with oil and arrange the zucchini close together. Bake in the oven for 35–40 minutes, until golden on top. Serve immediately. Garnish with oregano sprigs.

NUTRITION PER SERVE

Protein 12 g; Fat 10 g; Carbohydrate 10 g; Dietary Fibre 4.5 g; Cholesterol 73 mg; 758 kJ (180 Cal)

Cut the zucchini in half and scoop out the flesh with a teaspoon.

Combine the zucchini, bread, cheeses, herbs, garlic and egg yolk in a bowl.

Arrange the stuffed zucchini close together in the oiled baking dish.

Potato porcini bake

PREPARATION TIME: 30 MINUTES | TOTAL COOKING TIME: 45 MINUTES | SERVES 4–6

20 g (¾ oz) dried porcini mushrooms
185 ml (6 fl oz/¾ cup) hot milk
125 ml (4 fl oz/½ cup) pouring (whipping) cream
1 kg (2 lb 4 oz) waxy potatoes, unpeeled
30 g (1 oz) butter
1 garlic clove, crushed
60 g (2¼ oz) spring onions (scallions), sliced
120 g (4¼ oz/1 cup) grated fontina or gruyère cheese

1 Lightly brush a large shallow ovenproof dish with oil. Make sure the porcini are free of dirt or grit and put them in a bowl with the hot milk. Cover the bowl and set aside for 15 minutes. Remove the porcini, finely chop them and then return to the milk. Add the cream.

2 Meanwhile, slice the potatoes fairly thinly and cook in boiling salted water until just tender, then drain well. Melt the butter in a small saucepan and cook the garlic and spring onion until soft.

3 Preheat the oven to 180°C (350°F/Gas 4). Layer the potato in the dish with the garlic, spring onion and cheese, spooning the porcini mixture over each layer and seasoning with salt and freshly ground black pepper. Bake for 35 minutes, or until golden and tender. Serve hot.

NUTRITION PER SERVE (6)
Protein 10 g; Fat 20 g; Carbohydrate 25 g; Dietary Fibre 3 g; Cholesterol 65 mg; 1375 kJ (330 Cal)

Put the dried mushrooms in a bowl and leave to soak in the hot milk.

Layer the potato, spring onion and cheese in the dish, spooning the porcini over each layer.

Vegetable curry with spiced noodles

PREPARATION TIME: 40 MINUTES | TOTAL COOKING TIME: 35 MINUTES | SERVES 4–6

CURRY PASTE
5 red chillies, seeded and chopped
1 lemongrass stem, sliced
1 tablespoon chopped galangal
2 garlic cloves, crushed
1 small onion, chopped
1 tablespoon chopped coriander (cilantro)
10 black peppercorns
2 tablespoons lime juice
2 teaspoons oil

2 tablespoons oil
375 ml (13 fl oz/1½ cups) coconut milk
200 g (7 oz) green beans, cut into short lengths
2 small zucchini (courgettes), thickly sliced
1 eggplant (aubergine), cubed
5 makrut (kaffir lime) leaves
2 tablespoons lime juice
1 large handful chopped coriander (cilantro)
1 very large handful chopped basil

SPICED NOODLES
2 tablespoons oil
1 small onion, chopped
1 garlic clove, crushed
½–1 teaspoon dried chilli flakes
½ teaspoon garam masala
200 g (7 oz) thin egg noodles

1 To make the curry paste, blend all the ingredients in a food processor or blender to make a smooth paste.

2 Heat the oil in a pan and stir-fry the curry paste for 2 minutes. Add the coconut milk and 125 ml (4 fl oz/½ cup) water and bring to the boil. Reduce the heat and add the vegetables, makrut leaves and lime juice. Cook, covered, until tender. Add the coriander and basil.

3 To make the spiced noodles, heat the oil in a pan. Cook the onion and garlic over low heat for 5 minutes. Add the chilli flakes and garam masala and cook for 2 minutes. Meanwhile, cook the noodles in boiling water according to packet instructions, or until tender and drain. Add to the onion mixture and toss well. Serve with the vegetable curry.

NUTRITION PER SERVE (6)
Protein 5 g; Fat 25 g; Carbohydrate 15 g; Dietary Fibre 5 g; Cholesterol 0 mg; 1415 kJ (335 Cal)

Lemongrass and galangal are both available from Asian food stores.

Heat the oil in a saucepan and stir-fry the curry paste for 2 minutes.

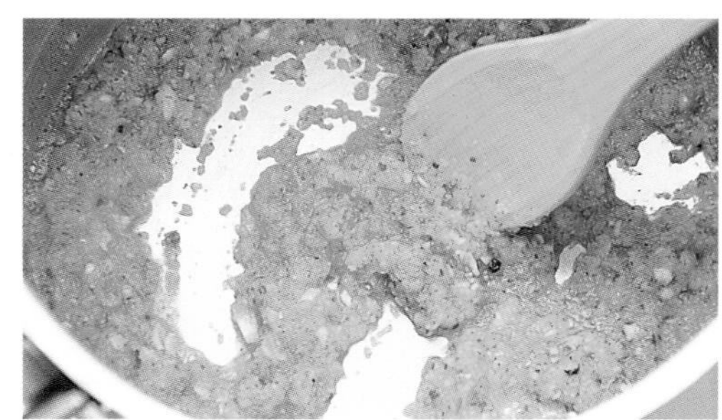

Add the noodles to a large saucepan of boiling water and cook until tender.

Mediterranean vegetable hotpot

PREPARATION TIME: 20 MINUTES | TOTAL COOKING TIME: 40 MINUTES | SERVES 4

3 tablespoons olive oil
1 onion, chopped
2 garlic cloves, crushed
1 green capsicum (pepper), chopped
1 red capsicum (pepper), chopped
3 zucchini (courgettes), sliced
3 slender eggplant (aubergine), sliced
440 g (15½ oz/2 cups) long-grain rice
250 ml (9 fl oz/1 cup) white wine
100 g (3½ oz) button mushrooms, sliced
750 ml (26 fl oz/3 cups) vegetable stock
400 g (14 oz) tin chopped tomatoes
2 tablespoons tomato paste (concentrated purée)
150 g (5½ oz) feta cheese

1 Heat the oil in a large heavy-based saucepan and cook the onion over medium heat for about 10 minutes, or until very soft but not browned. Add the garlic and cook for a further minute.

2 Add the green and red capsicums and cook, stirring, for 3 minutes, Add the zucchini and eggplant and stir-fry for a further 5 minutes. Add the rice and stir-fry for 2 minutes.

3 Add the wine, mushrooms, stock, chopped tomatoes and tomato paste. Stir to combine. Bring to the boil, reduce the heat, cover and simmer for 20 minutes. The rice should be tender. Serve immediately, topped with the crumbled feta cheese.

NOTE: *Like most hotpots and casseroles, this is best made a day in advance to let the flavours develop.*

Add the zucchini and eggplant to the pan and stir-fry for a little longer.

Add the wine, mushrooms, stock, chopped tomatoes and tomato paste.

NUTRITION PER SERVE
Protein 20 g; Fat 25 g; Carbohydrate 92 g; Dietary Fibre 9 g; Cholesterol 25 mg; 2980 kJ (710 Cal)

Roman gnocchi

PREPARATION TIME: 15 MINUTES + 1 HOUR REFRIGERATION | TOTAL COOKING TIME: 40 MINUTES | SERVES 4

750 ml (26 fl oz/3 cups) milk
½ teaspoon ground nutmeg
90 g (3¼ oz/¾ cup) semolina
1 egg, beaten
150 g (5½ oz/1½ cups) grated parmesan cheese
60 g (2¼ oz) butter, melted
125 ml (4 fl oz/½ cup) pouring (whipping) cream
60 g (2¼ oz/½ cup) grated mozzarella cheese

1 Line a deep 30 x 20 cm (12 x 8 inch) Swiss roll tin with baking paper. Put the milk, half the nutmeg and some salt and freshly ground black pepper in a saucepan and bring to the boil. Reduce the heat and gradually stir in the semolina. Cook, stirring occasionally, for 5–10 minutes, or until the semolina is very stiff.

2 Remove from the heat. Add the egg and 100 g (3½ oz/1 cup) parmesan and stir well. Spread into the tin and refrigerate for 1 hour, or until firm.

3 Preheat the oven to 180°C (350°F/Gas 4). Cut the semolina into rounds with a floured 4 cm (1½ inch) cutter. Arrange in a greased shallow casserole dish.

4 Pour the butter over the top and then the cream. Sprinkle with the combined remaining parmesan and mozzarella cheeses. Sprinkle with the remaining nutmeg. Bake for 20–25 minutes, or until golden.

NOTE: *Roman gnocchi is also known as gnocchi alla semolina, to differentiate it from the small potato gnocchi that are boiled and served with pasta sauce.*

Use a floured biscuit cutter to cut the gnocchi into circles.

Mix together the grated parmesan and mozzarella and sprinkle over the gnocchi.

NUTRITION PER SERVE
Protein 33 g; Fat 53 g; Carbohydrate 24 g; Dietary Fibre 0.5 g; Cholesterol 205 mg; 2918 kJ (697 Cal)

Three-bean chilli

PREPARATION TIME: 20 MINUTES + 2 HOURS STANDING | TOTAL COOKING TIME: 1 HOUR 35 MINUTES | SERVES 4

220 g (7¾ oz/1 cup) dried black beans (see NOTE)
2 tablespoons oil
1 large onion, finely chopped
3 garlic cloves, crushed
2 tablespoons ground cumin
1 tablespoon ground coriander
1 teaspoon ground cinnamon
1 teaspoon chilli powder
400 g (14 oz) tin chopped tomatoes
375 ml (13 fl oz/1½ cups) vegetable stock
400 g (14 oz) tin chickpeas, drained and rinsed
400 g (14 oz) tin red kidney beans, drained and rinsed
2 tablespoons tomato paste (concentrated purée)
1 tablespoon sugar
sour cream and corn chips, to serve

1 Place the black beans in a large saucepan, cover with water and bring to the boil. Turn off the heat and set aside for 2 hours. Drain he beans, cover with fresh water and boil for 1 hour, until the beans are tender but not mushy. Drain well.

2 Heat the oil in a large saucepan and cook the onion over low-medium heat for 5 minutes, until golden, stirring frequently. Reduce the heat, add the garlic and spices and stir for 1 minute.

3 Add the tomatoes, stock, chickpeas, kidney beans and black beans and combine with the onion mixture. Bring to the boil, then simmer for 20 minutes, stirring occasionally.

4 Add the tomato paste, sugar and season to taste. Simmer for a further 5 minutes. Serve with sour cream and corn chips on the side.

NOTE: *If black beans are unavailable, double the quantity of kidney beans and chickpeas. Do not confuse black beans with Asian black beans, which are fermented soy.*

NUTRITION PER SERVE
Protein 40 g; Fat 55 g; Carbohydrate 125 g; Dietary Fibre 36 g; Cholesterol 40 mg; 4775 kJ (1140 Cal)

Cook the chopped onion, stirring frequently, until it turns golden.

Add the tomatoes, stock, chickpeas, kidney beans and black beans to the saucepan.

Add salt and pepper to taste and simmer the chilli for a further 5 minutes.

Chickpea curry

PREPARATION TIME: 10 MINUTES | COOKING TIME: 40 MINUTES | SERVES 4

1 tablespoon ghee or oil
2 onions, sliced
4 garlic cloves, crushed
1 teaspoon chilli powder
1 teaspoon ground turmeric
1 teaspoon paprika
1 tablespoon ground cumin
1 tablespoon ground coriander
880 g (1 lb 15 oz) tin chickpeas, drained and rinsed
440 g (14 oz) tin chopped tomatoes
1 teaspoon garam masala

1 Heat the ghee or oil in a saucepan. Add the onion and garlic and cook, stirring, until the onion is soft. Add the chilli powder, 1 teaspoon of salt, turmeric, paprika, cumin and coriander. Cook, stirring, for 2–3 minutes.

2 Stir in the chickpeas and tomato. Simmer, covered, over low heat for 20 minutes, stirring occasionally.

3 Stir in the garam masala. Simmer, covered, for a further 10 minutes. Serve with naan bread.

NUTRITION PER SERVE
Protein 45 g; Fat 20 g; Carbohydrate 120 g; Dietary Fibre 35 g; Cholesterol 15 mg; 3315 kJ (790 Cal)

Add the chilli powder, salt, turmeric, paprika, cumin and coriander to the pan.

Add the rinsed and drained chickpeas, and chopped tomatoes.

Stir in 1 teaspoon of garam masala and then simmer, covered, for 10 minutes.

Tomato and potato stew

PREPARATION TIME: 30 MINUTES | TOTAL COOKING TIME: 1 HOUR 15 MINUTES | SERVES 6

3 tablespoons olive oil
2 red capsicums (peppers), chopped
2 green capsicums (peppers), chopped
3 onions, thinly sliced
4 garlic cloves, crushed
2 x 400 g (14 oz) tins chopped tomatoes
3–4 sprigs thyme, plus extra, to garnish
2 bay leaves
2 teaspoons caster (superfine) sugar
1.2 kg (2 lb 7 oz) potatoes, cut into chunks
125 g (4½ oz/1 cup) black olives, pitted
parmesan cheese shavings, to serve

1 Heat the oil in a large, heavy-based saucepan. When the oil is hot, cook the capsicum, onion and garlic over medium heat for 10 minutes, or until softened. Add the chopped tomatoes, 125 ml (4 fl oz) water, thyme sprigs, bay leaves and sugar. Season with salt and freshly ground black pepper to taste and leave to simmer gently for 15 minutes.

2 Add the potato chunks, cover and cook very gently for about an hour, or until tender. Stir in the olives. Garnish with the parmesan shavings and thyme sprigs.

NUTRITION PER SERVE
Protein 10 g; Fat 12 g; Carbohydrate 40 g; Dietary Fibre 9 g; Cholesterol 3 mg; 1330 kJ (320 Cal)

When the oil is hot, fry the capsicum, onion and garlic until soft.

Add the chunks of potato to the tomato mixture and cook very gently until tender.

The easiest way to make parmesan shavings is to run a vegetable peeler over a block.

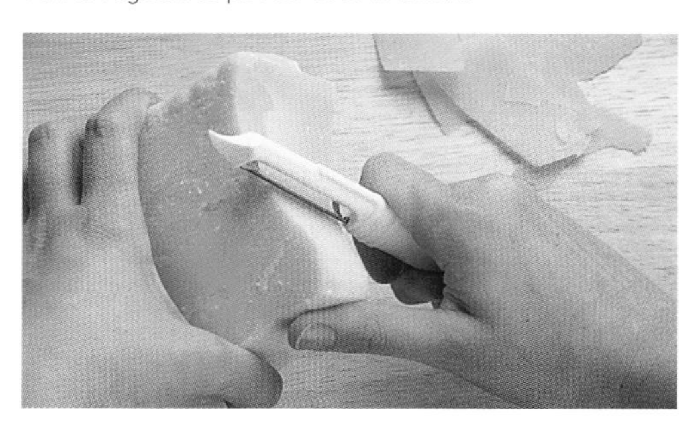

Spicy vegetable stew with dhal

PREPARATION TIME: 25 MINUTES + 2 HOURS SOAKING | TOTAL COOKING TIME: 1 HOUR 35 MINUTES | SERVES 4–6

DHAL
165 g (5¾ oz/¾ cup) yellow split peas
5 cm (2 inch) piece of fresh ginger, grated
2–3 garlic cloves, crushed
1 red chilli, seeded and chopped

3 tomatoes
2 tablespoons oil
1 teaspoon yellow mustard seeds
1 teaspoon cumin seeds
1 teaspoon ground cumin
½ teaspoon garam masala
1 red onion, cut into thin wedges
3 slender eggplants (aubergines), thickly sliced
2 carrots, thickly sliced
¼ cauliflower, cut into florets
375 ml (13 fl oz/1½ cups) vegetable stock
2 small zucchini (courgettes), thickly sliced
90 g (3¼ oz/½ cup) frozen peas
1 large handful coriander (cilantro) leaves

1 To make the dhal, put the split peas in a bowl, cover with water and soak for 2 hours. Drain. Place in a large saucepan with the ginger, garlic, chilli and 750 ml (26 fl oz/3 cups) water. Bring to the boil, reduce the heat and simmer for 45 minutes, or until soft.

2 Score a cross in the base of each tomato, soak in boiling water for 30 seconds, then plunge into cold water and peel the skin away from the cross. Cut in half and scoop out the seeds with a teaspoon. Chop the tomato flesh.

3 Heat the oil in a large saucepan. Cook the spices over medium heat for 30 seconds, or until fragrant. Add the onion and cook for 2 minutes, or until the onion is soft. Stir in the tomato, eggplant, carrot and cauliflower.

4 Add the dhal and stock, mix together well and simmer, covered, for 45 minutes, or until the vegetables are tender. Stir occasionally. Add the zucchini and peas during the last 10 minutes of cooking. Stir in the coriander leaves and serve hot.

NUTRITION PER SERVE (6)
Protein 11 g; Fat 7 g; Carbohydrate 20 g; Dietary Fibre 8.5 g; Cholesterol 17 mg; 780 kJ (186 Cal)

Simmer the dhal for 45 minutes, or until the split peas are soft.

Score a cross in the top of each tomato, then soak in hot water to make the skin come away.

Add the dhal and stock to the stew and simmer for 45 minutes, or until the vegetables are tender.

Spicy beans on baked sweet potato

PREPARATION TIME: 20 MINUTES | TOTAL COOKING TIME: 1 HOUR 30 MINUTES | SERVES 6

3 orange sweet potatoes
1 tablespoon olive oil
1 large onion, chopped
3 garlic cloves, crushed
2 teaspoons ground cumin
1 teaspoon ground coriander
½ teaspoon chilli powder
400 g (14 oz) tin chopped tomatoes
250 ml (9 fl oz/1 cup) vegetable stock
1 large zucchini (courgette), cut into squares
1 green capsicum (pepper), cubed
310 g (11 oz) tin corn kernels, drained
2 x 400 g (14 oz) tins red kidney beans, drained and rinsed
3 tablespoons chopped coriander (cilantro) leaves
sour cream and grated cheddar cheese, to serve

1 Preheat the oven to 210°C (415°F/Gas 6–7). Rinse the sweet potatoes, then pierce with a sharp knife. Place on a baking tray and bake for 1–1½ hours, or until soft when tested with a skewer.

2 Meanwhile, heat the oil in a large saucepan and cook the onion over medium heat for 5 minutes, stirring occasionally, until very soft. Add the garlic and spices, and cook, stirring, for 1 minute.

3 Add the tomato and stock, stir well, then add vegetables and beans. Bring to the boil, then reduce the heat and simmer, partially covered, for 20 minutes. Uncover, increase heat slightly, and cook for a further 10–15 minutes, or until liquid has reduced and thickened. Stir in the coriander leaves just before serving.To serve, cut the sweet potatoes in half lengthways. Spoon the mixture over the top. Add a dollop of sour cream and sprinkle with grated cheddar cheese.

Cook the spicy vegetable mixture until the liquid has reduced.

Cut the baked sweet potatoes in half lengthways and top with the spicy beans.

NUTRITION PER SERVE
Protein 15 g; Fat 5 g; Carbohydrate 72 g; Dietary Fibre 17 g; Cholesterol 0 mg; 1665 kJ (397 Cal)

Eggplant parmigiana

PREPARATION TIME: 30 MINUTES | TOTAL COOKING TIME: 1 HOUR 15 MINUTES | SERVES 6–8

3 tablespoons olive oil, plus extra, for shallow-frying
1 onion, diced
2 garlic cloves, crushed
1.25 kg (2 lb 12 oz) tomatoes, peeled and chopped
1 kg (2 lb 4 oz) eggplants (aubergines)
250 g (9 oz) bocconcini (fresh baby mozzarella cheese), sliced
185 g (6½ oz) cheddar cheese, finely grated
2 large handfuls basil leaves
50 g (1¾ oz/½ cup) grated parmesan

1 Heat the oil in a large frying pan, add the onion and cook over moderate heat until soft. Add the garlic and cook for 1 minute. Add the tomato and simmer for 15 minutes. Season with salt to taste. Set aside and keep warm. Preheat the oven to 200°C (400°F/Gas 6).

2 Slice the eggplants very thinly and shallow-fry in a separate frying pan in oil in batches for 3–4 minutes, or until golden brown. Drain on paper towels.

3 Place one-third of the eggplant in a 1.75 litre (60 fl oz/7 cup) ovenproof dish. Top with half the bocconcini and cheddar. Repeat the layers, finishing with a layer of eggplant.

4 Pour the tomato mixture over the eggplant. Scatter with torn basil leaves, then parmesan. Bake for 40 minutes.

VARIATION: *If you prefer not to fry the eggplant, brush it lightly with oil and brown lightly under a hot grill (broiler).*

Shallow-fry the eggplant in batches, then drain on paper towels.

Arrange layers of eggplant, bocconcini and cheddar in the dish.

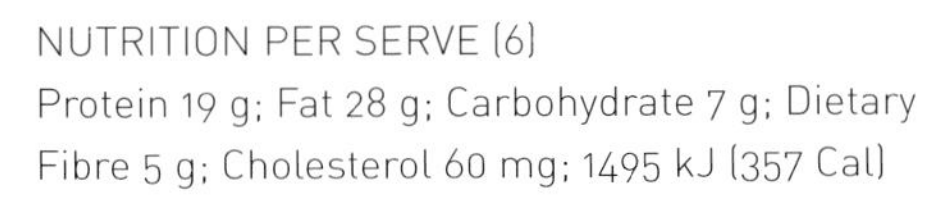

NUTRITION PER SERVE (6)
Protein 19 g; Fat 28 g; Carbohydrate 7 g; Dietary Fibre 5 g; Cholesterol 60 mg; 1495 kJ (357 Cal)

Moroccan tagine with couscous

PREPARATION TIME: 20 MINUTES | TOTAL COOKING TIME: 1 HOUR | SERVES 4–6

2 tablespoons oil
2 onions, chopped
1 teaspoon ground ginger
2 teaspoons ground paprika
2 teaspoons ground cumin
1 cinnamon stick
pinch of saffron threads
1.5 kg (3 lb 5 oz) vegetables, peeled and cut into large chunks (carrot, eggplant (aubergine), orange sweet potato, parsnip, potato, pumpkin (winter squash))
½ preserved lemon, rinsed, pith and flesh removed, thinly sliced
400 g (14 oz) tin peeled tomatoes
250 ml (9 fl oz/1 cup) vegetable stock
100 g (3½ oz) dried pears, halved
60 g (2¼ oz) pitted prunes
2 zucchini (courgettes), cut into large chunks
300 g (10½ oz) instant couscous
1 tablespoon olive oil
3 tablespoons chopped flat-leaf (Italian) parsley
50 g (1¾ oz/⅓ cup) almonds, toasted

1 Preheat the oven to 180°C (350°F/Gas 4). Heat the oil in a large saucepan or ovenproof dish, add the onion and cook over medium heat for 5 minutes, or until soft. Add the spices and cook for 3 minutes.

2 Add the vegetables and cook, stirring, until coated with the spices and the outside begins to soften. Add the preserved lemon, tomato, stock, pear and prune. Cover, transfer to the oven and cook for 30 minutes. Add the zucchini and cook for 15–20 minutes, or until the vegetables are tender.

3 Cover the couscous with the olive oil and 500 ml (17 fl oz/2 cups) boiling water and leave until all the water has been absorbed. Flake with a fork.

4 Remove the cinnamon stick from the vegetables, then stir in the parsley. Serve on a large platter with the couscous formed into a ring and the vegetable tagine in the centre, sprinkled with the almonds.

NUTRITION PER SERVE (6)
Protein 8 g; Fat 15 g; Carbohydrate 33 g; Dietary Fibre 9 g; Cholesterol 0 mg; 1240 kJ (296 Cal)

Cook the vegetables until they are coated in spices and the outside starts to soften.

Once all the water has been absorbed, flake the couscous with a fork.

Before serving, remove the cinnamon stick with a pair of tongs.

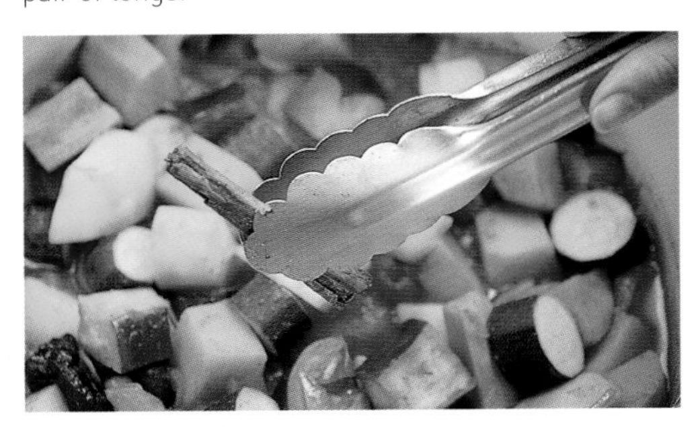

Potato gratin

PREPARATION TIME: 25 MINUTES | TOTAL COOKING TIME: 1 HOUR | SERVES 4

30 g (1 oz) butter
1 onion, halved and thinly sliced
650 g (1 lb 7 oz) floury potatoes, thinly sliced
90 g (3¼ oz/⅔ cup) grated cheddar cheese
300 ml (10½ fl oz) pouring (whipping) cream
100 ml (3½ fl oz) milk

1 Heat the butter in a frying pan and cook the onion over low heat for 5 minutes, or until it is soft and translucent.

2 Preheat the oven to 160°C (315°F/Gas 3). Grease the base and sides of a deep 1 litre (35 fl oz/4 cup) ovenproof dish. Layer the potato slices with the onion and cheese (reserving 2 tablespoons of cheese for the top). Whisk together the cream and milk, and season with salt and freshly ground black pepper. Slowly pour over the potato, then sprinkle with the remaining cheese.

3 Bake for 50–60 minutes, or until golden brown and the potato is very soft. Leave to rest for 10 minutes before serving.

VARIATION: *For something different, try combining potato and orange sweet potato, layering alternately. For extra flavour, add chopped fresh herbs to the cream and milk mixture.*

NUTRITION PER SERVE
Protein 12 g; Fat 50 g; Carbohydrate 25 g; Dietary Fibre 3 g; Cholesterol 155 mg; 2465 kJ (590 Cal)

Peel the onion and slice it in half before cutting into thin slices.

Use a large sharp knife to cut the potatoes into thin, even slices.

Add the onion to the butter and cook, stirring occasionally, until soft and translucent.

Curried lentils

PREPARATION TIME: 15 MINUTES | TOTAL COOKING TIME: 30 MINUTES | SERVES 4

250 g (9 oz/1 cup) red lentils
500 ml (17 fl oz/2 cups) vegetable stock
½ teaspoon ground turmeric
50 g (1¾ oz) ghee
1 onion, chopped
2 garlic cloves, finely chopped
1 large green chilli, seeded and finely chopped
2 teaspoons ground cumin
2 teaspoons ground coriander
2 tomatoes, chopped
125 ml (4 fl oz/½ cup) coconut milk

1 Rinse the lentils and drain well. Place the lentils, stock and turmeric in a large heavy-based saucepan. Bring to the boil, reduce the heat and simmer, covered, for 10 minutes, or until just tender. Stir occasionally and check the mixture is not catching on the bottom of the pan.

2 Meanwhile, heat the ghee in a small frying pan and add the onion. Cook until soft and golden and add the garlic, chilli, cumin and coriander. Cook, stirring, for 2–3 minutes until fragrant. Stir the onions and spices into the lentil mixture and then add the tomato. Simmer over very low heat for 5 minutes, stirring frequently.

3 Season to taste and add the coconut milk. Stir until heated through. Serve with rice or naan bread.

NUTRITION PER SERVE
Protein 15 g; Fat 20 g; Carbohydrate 25 g; Dietary Fibre 10 g; Cholesterol 35 mg; 1500 kJ (355 Cal)

Add the chopped tomato and simmer over very low heat for 5 minutes.

Season the lentils and add the coconut milk. Stir until heated through.

Mushroom nut roast with tomato sauce

PREPARATION TIME: 25 MINUTES | TOTAL COOKING TIME: 50 MINUTES | SERVES 6

- 2 tablespoons olive oil
- 1 large onion, diced
- 2 garlic cloves, crushed
- 300 g (10½ oz) cap mushrooms, finely chopped
- 200 g (7 oz) cashew nuts
- 200 g (7 oz) Brazil nuts
- 125 g (4½ oz/1 cup) grated cheddar cheese
- 30 g (1 oz) parmesan cheese, grated
- 1 egg, lightly beaten
- 2 tablespoons snipped chives
- 80 g (2¾ oz/1 cup) fresh wholemeal (whole-wheat) breadcrumbs

TOMATO SAUCE
- 1½ tablespoons olive oil
- 1 onion, finely chopped
- 1 garlic clove, crushed
- 400 g (14 oz) tin chopped tomatoes
- 1 tablespoon tomato paste (concentrated purée)
- 1 teaspoon caster (superfine) sugar

1 Preheat the oven to 180°C (350°F/Gas 4). Grease a 15 x 20 cm (6 x 8 inch) baking tin and line with baking paper. Heat the oil in a frying pan and fry the onion, garlic and mushrooms over medium heat for 2–3 minutes, or until soft. Cool.

2 Finely chop the nuts in a food processor, but do not overprocess.

3 Combine the nuts, mushroom mixture, cheeses, egg, chives and breadcrumbs in a bowl. Press into the tin and bake for 45 minutes until firm. Leave for 5 minutes, then turn out.

4 Meanwhile, to make the tomato sauce, heat the oil in a frying pan and add the onion and garlic. Cook over low heat for 5 minutes, or until soft. Add the tomato, tomato paste, sugar and 4 tablespoons of water. Simmer for 3–5 minutes, or until thick. Season. Serve with the sliced roast.

NUTRITION PER SERVE
Protein 18 g; Fat 44 g; Carbohydrate 16 g; Dietary Fibre 6.5 g; Cholesterol 55 mg; 2195 kJ (525 Cal)

Finely chop the cashew nuts and Brazil nuts in a food processor, but don't overprocess.

Press the nutty mushroom mixture into the prepared tin.

Simmer the tomato sauce for 3–5 minutes, or until thickened.

Soya bean moussaka

PREPARATION TIME: 25 MINUTES | TOTAL COOKING TIME: 1 HOUR | SERVES 4

2 eggplants (aubergines)
1 tablespoon oil
1 onion, finely chopped
2 garlic cloves, crushed
2 ripe tomatoes, peeled, seeded and chopped
2 teaspoons tomato paste (concentrated purée)
½ teaspoon dried oregano
125 ml (4 fl oz/½ cup) dry white wine
300 g (10½ oz) tin soya beans, drained and rinsed
3 tablespoons chopped flat-leaf (Italian) parsley
30 g (1 oz) butter
2 tablespoons plain (all-purpose) flour
pinch of ground nutmeg
310 ml (10¾ fl oz/1¼ cups) milk
40 g (1½ oz/⅓ cup) grated cheddar cheese

1 Preheat the oven to 180°C (350°F/Gas 4). Cut eggplants in half lengthways. Spoon out flesh, leaving a narrow border and place on a large baking tray, cut side up. Use crumpled foil around the sides of the eggplant to support it.

2 Heat the oil in a large frying pan. Cook onion and garlic over medium heat for 3 minutes, or until soft. Add tomato, paste, oregano and wine. Boil for 3 minutes, or until liquid is reduced and tomato is soft. Stir in the soya beans and parsley.

3 To make sauce, melt butter in a saucepan. Stir in flour and cook over medium heat for 1 minute, or until foamy. Remove from heat and gradually stir in nutmeg and milk. Return to heat; stir constantly until sauce boils and thickens. Pour one-third of sauce into mixture and stir.

4 Spoon mixture into eggplant shells. Smooth before spreading remaining sauce evenly over the top and sprinkling with cheese. Bake for 50 minutes, or until cooked through. Serve hot.

Scoop out the eggplant flesh, leaving a narrow border all the way around.

Add the soya beans and parsley to the tomato mixture and stir well.

NUTRITION PER SERVE

Protein 35 g; Fat 33 g; Carbohydrate 20 g; Dietary Fibre 20 g; Cholesterol 40 mg; 2192 kJ (524 Cal)

Dry potato and pea curry

PREPARATION TIME: 15 MINUTES | TOTAL COOKING TIME: 20–25 MINUTES | SERVES 4

2 teaspoons brown mustard seeds
2 tablespoons ghee or oil
2 onions, sliced
2 garlic cloves, crushed
2 teaspoons grated fresh ginger
1 teaspoon ground turmeric
½ teaspoon chilli powder
1 teaspoon ground cumin
1 teaspoon garam masala
750 g (1 lb 10 oz) potatoes, cubed
100 g (3½ oz/⅔ cup) peas
2 tablespoons chopped mint

1 Heat the mustard seeds in a dry pan until they start to pop. Add the ghee, onion, garlic and ginger and cook, stirring, until the onion is soft.

2 Add the turmeric, chilli powder, cumin, garam marsala and potato, and season with salt and freshly ground black pepper. Stir until the potato is coated with the spice mixture. Add 125ml (4 fl oz/½ cup) water and simmer, covered, for about 15–20 minutes, or until the potato is just tender. Stir occasionally to stop the curry sticking to the bottom of the pan.

3 Add the peas and stir until well combined. Simmer, covered, for 3–5 minutes, or until the potato is cooked and all the liquid is absorbed. Stir in the mint and season well.

Fry the mustard seeds in a dry frying pan until they begin to pop.

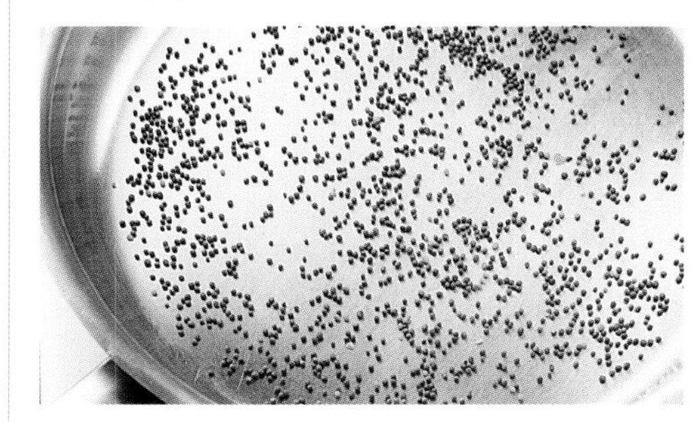

Stir in the chopped mint before seasoning with salt and pepper, to taste.

NUTRITION PER SERVE
Protein 5 g; Fat 10 g; Carbohydrate 30 g; Dietary Fibre 5 g; Cholesterol 25 mg; 985 kJ (235 Cal)

Lentil and cauliflower curry stacks

PREPARATION TIME: 15 MINUTES | TOTAL COOKING TIME: 50 MINUTES | SERVES 6

60 g (2¼ oz) ghee or butter
2 onions, thinly sliced
2 tablespoons madras curry paste
2 garlic cloves, crushed
180 g (6 oz) button mushrooms, sliced
1 litre (35 fl oz/4 cups) vegetable stock
300 g (10½ oz) brown or green lentils
400 g (14 oz) tin chopped tomatoes
2 cinnamon sticks
300 g (10½ oz) cauliflower, cut into small florets
oil, for deep-frying
18 small (8 cm/3¼ inch) pappadums
plain yoghurt and coriander (cilantro) sprigs, to serve

NUTRITION PER SERVE
Protein 16 g; Fat 13 g; Carbohydrate 23 g; Dietary Fibre 10 g; Cholesterol 24 mg; 1144 kJ (273 Cal)

1 Heat the ghee in a large saucepan over medium heat and cook the onion for 2–3 minutes, or until soft. Add the curry paste, garlic and mushrooms and cook for 2 minutes, or until soft.

2 Add the stock, lentils, tomato and cinnamon sticks and mix well. Bring to the boil and cook for 40 minutes, or until the lentils are tender. Add the cauliflower in the last 10 minutes and cover. If the curry is too wet, continue to cook, uncovered, until the excess liquid has evaporated. Season to taste with salt and freshly ground black pepper. Remove the cinnamon.

3 Meanwhile, fill a deep, heavy-based saucepan one-third full of oil and heat until a cube of bread dropped into the oil browns in 15 seconds. Cook the pappadums in batches for 10 seconds, or until golden brown and puffed all over. Drain on crumpled paper towels and season with salt.

4 To assemble, place a pappadum on each serving plate and spoon on a little of the curry. Place a second pappadum on top and spoon on some more curry. Cover with the remaining pappadum and top with a spoonful of yoghurt. Garnish with coriander sprigs and serve immediately (the pappadums will become soggy if left to stand for too long).

If the curry is too wet, continue cooking to evaporate the excess liquid.

Drop the pappadums into the oil and cook until puffed and golden.

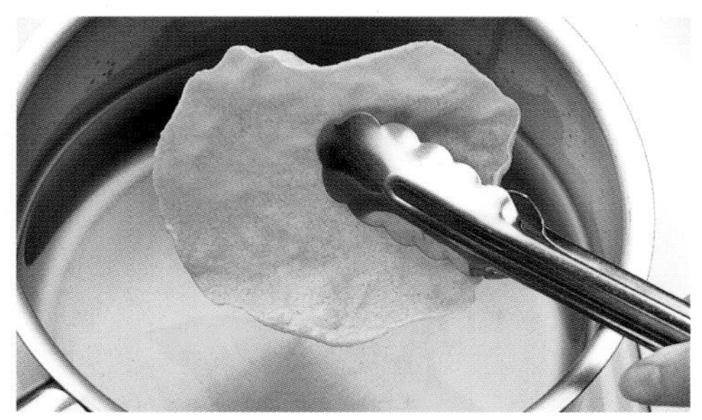

Cauliflower cheese

PREPARATION TIME: 15 MINUTES | TOTAL COOKING TIME: 20 MINUTES | SERVES 4

500 g (1 lb 2 oz) cauliflower, cut into pieces
30 g (1 oz) butter
30 g (1 oz) plain (all-purpose) flour
310 ml (10¾ fl oz/1¼ cups) warm milk
1 teaspoon dijon mustard
60 g (2¼ oz/½ cup) grated cheddar cheese
60 g (2¼ oz/½ cup) grated parmesan cheese
2 tablespoons fresh breadcrumbs
3 tablespoons grated cheddar, extra

1 Brush a 1.5 litre (52 fl oz/6 cup) ovenproof dish with melted butter or oil. Cook the cauliflower in lightly salted boiling water until just tender. Drain. Place in the dish and keep warm.

2 Melt the butter in a saucepan. Stir in the flour and cook for 1 minute, or until golden and bubbling. Remove from the heat and whisk in the milk and mustard. Return to the heat and bring to the boil, stirring constantly. Cook, stirring, over low heat for 2 minutes, then remove from the heat. Add the cheeses and stir until melted. Season with salt and white pepper and pour over the cauliflower.

3 Mix together the breadcrumbs and extra cheddar cheese and sprinkle over the sauce. Grill (broil) until the top is browned and bubbling. Serve immediately.

NUTRITION PER SERVE
Protein 22 g; Fat 33 g; Carbohydrate 15 g; Dietary Fibre 2 g; Cholesterol 88 mg; 1840 kJ (440 Cal)

Add the cheddar and parmesan and stir until the cheeses have melted.

Oven-baked potato, leek and olives

PREPARATION TIME: 20 MINUTES | TOTAL COOKING TIME: 1 HOUR | SERVES 4–6

2 tablespoons extra virgin olive oil
1 leek, finely sliced
375 ml (13 fl oz/1½ cups) vegetable stock
2 teaspoons chopped thyme
1 kg (2 lb 4 oz) potatoes, unpeeled, cut into thin slices
6–8 pitted black olives, sliced
60 g (2¼ oz/½ cup) grated parmesan cheese
30 g (1 oz) butter, chopped

1 Preheat the oven to 180°C (350°F/Gas 4). Brush a shallow 1.25 litre (44 fl oz/5 cup) ovenproof dish with a little olive oil. Heat the remaining oil in a large saucepan and cook the leek over moderate heat until soft. Add the stock, thyme and potato. Cover and leave to simmer for 5 minutes.

2 Using tongs, lift out half the potato and put in the ovenproof dish. Sprinkle with olives and parmesan and season with salt and freshly ground black pepper.

3 Layer with the remaining potato, then spoon the leek and stock mixture in at the side of the dish, keeping the top dry.

4 Scatter chopped butter over the potato and then bake, uncovered, for 50 minutes, or until cooked and golden brown. Leave in a warm place for about 10 minutes before serving.

NOTE: *Keeping the top layer of potato dry as you pour in the stock mixture will give the dish a crisp finish.*

NUTRITION PER SERVE (6)
Protein 7.5 g; Fat 13 g; Carbohydrate 23 g; Dietary Fibre 3 g; Cholesterol 20 mg; 1019 kJ (243 Cal)

Spoon the leek and stock mixture around the side, trying to keep the top dry.

Bake, uncovered, until the potatoes on top are golden brown.

Basics—pestos, oils and more

Pestos & tapenades

Red pesto

SERVES 375 ML [13 FL OZ/1½ CUPS]

Put a 200 g (7 oz) jar sun-dried tomatoes in oil, 1 small handful of basil leaves, 1 small handful flat-leaf (Italian) parsley, 2 chopped garlic cloves, 2 teaspoons drained and rinsed capers and 4 tablespoons lightly toasted pine nuts in a food processor or blender. Process until finely minced. Keep the motor running while you pour in 2 tablespoons red wine vinegar and 125 ml (4 fl oz/½ cup) extra virgin olive oil. When these are thoroughly blended, add 2 tablespoons freshly grated parmesan cheese and some freshly ground black pepper. Sterilise a jar with boiling water, then dry in a warm oven. Do not dry with a tea towel (dish towel). Transfer the pesto to the sterilised jar. Seal and refrigerate for up to 4 days. Serve as a pasta sauce if thinned with a little more olive oil, or a dip for crudités.

Rocket and pecan pesto

SERVES 310 ML [10¾ FL OZ/1¼ CUPS]

Combine 60 g (2¼ oz) young rocket (arugula) leaves, 1 small handful flat-leaf (Italian) parsley, 12 large pecan halves and 2 coarsely chopped large garlic cloves in a food processor or blender. With the motor running, slowly pour in 125 ml (4 fl oz/½ cup) extra virgin olive oil. Add 35 g (1¼ oz/1⁄3 cup) freshly grated parmesan and mix well. Lightly season with salt. Sterilise a jar with boiling water, then dry in a warm oven. Do not dry with a tea towel (dish towel). Put the pesto in the sterilised jar. Seal and refrigerate for 3 days. Serve as a dip with crudités and crusty bread, or as a pasta sauce.

Traditional pesto

SERVES 250 ML [9 FL OZ/1 CUP]

Whiz 2 very large handfuls of basil leaves, 40 g (1½ oz/¼ cup) lightly toasted pine nuts, 2 coarsely grated chopped large garlic cloves and a pinch of salt in a food processor or blender. With the motor running, slowly pour in 4 tablespoons extra virgin olive oil. Add 50 g (1¾ oz/½ cup) freshly grated parmesan cheese and some freshly ground black pepper and process until just combined. Sterilise a jar with boiling water, then dry in a warm oven. Do not dry with a tea towel (dish towel). Transfer the pesto to the sterilised jar. Seal and refrigerate for up 3 days. Serve as a pasta sauce or a dip.

North African tapenade

SERVES 185 ML [6 FL OZ/¾ CUP]

Put a pinch of saffron threads in a small bowl with 1 teaspoon hot water and set aside. Whiz 140 g (5 oz/⅔ cup) pitted green olives, ¼ teaspoon dried oregano, 2 tablespoons toasted pine nuts, 1 chopped garlic clove and ⅛ teaspoon ground cumin in a food processor or blender. With the motor running, add 3 teaspoons lime juice, 3 tablespoons extra virgin olive oil and the saffron and water mixture. Stop processing as soon as the ingredients are blended. Sterilise a jar with boiling water, then dry in a warm over. Do not dry with a tea towel (dish towel). Transfer the tapenade to a sterilised jar. Seal and store in the refrigerator for up to 1 week. Delicious as a pasta sauce when thinned with a little more oil.

Olive tapenade

SERVES 250 ML [9 FL OZ/1 CUP]

Place 1 tablespoon drained and rinsed capers, 1 small garlic clove, 125 g (4½ oz/1 cup) sliced pitted black or green olives and 2 tablespoons lemon juice in a food processor or blender. While the motor is running, pour in 2 tablespoons extra virgin olive oil and 1½ tablespoons cognac. Season to taste with freshly ground black pepper. Sterilise a jar with boiling water, then dry in a warm oven. Transfer the tapenade to the sterilised jar. Seal and refrigerate for up to 1 week. Serve as a spread for bread or with crudités.

Oils & vinegars

Chilli oil

SERVES 750 ML [26 FL OZ/3 CUPS]

Place 6 dried chillies and 1 teaspoon of chilli powder in a heavy-based pan. Add 750 ml (26 fl oz/3 cups) olive oil, bring to the boil, then lower the heat and simmer for 5 minutes (if it gets too hot the oil will change flavour). Cover with plastic wrap and leave in a cool, dark place for 3 days. Strain the oil into a 750 ml (26 fl oz/3 cup) sterilised bottle. Discard the chillies and add new chillies for decoration. Store in a cool dark place for up to 6 months.

Indian oil

SERVES 750 ML [26 FL OZ/3 CUPS]

Place 1 teaspoon each of garam masala, coriander seeds, cardamom pods and fennel seeds, 3 allspice berries, 3 curry leaves and 1 small dried chilli in a bowl and lightly crush with the back of a spoon. Place in a sterilised bottle with 750 ml (26 fl oz/3 cups) peanut or canola oil. Seal and leave for 3 days in a cool, dark place. Strain into a 750 ml (26 fl oz/3 cup) sterilised bottle. Store in a cool dark place for up to 3 months.

Parmesan oil

SERVES 500 ML [17 FL OZ/2 CUPS]

Combine 500 ml (17 fl oz/2 cups) olive oil and 100 g (3½ oz) finely grated reggiano parmesan cheese in a small saucepan. Stir over low heat for 10-15 minutes, or until the parmesan starts to melt and clump together. Remove from the heat and allow to cool. Strain into a 500 ml (17 fl oz/2 cups) sterilised bottle and add 20 g (¾ oz) shaved parmesan. Seal and label. Store in a cool, dark place for up to 6 months.

Raspberry vinegar

SERVES 500 ML [17 FL OZ/2 CUPS]

Place 290 g (10¼ oz/2½ cups) fresh or thawed frozen raspberries in a non-metallic bowl and crush gently with the back of a spoon. Over low heat, warms 500 ml (17 fl oz/2 cups) white wine vinegar. Add the vinegar to the raspberries and mix well. Pour into a 500 ml (17 fl oz/2 cups) sterilised jar and keep in a warm place for 2 weeks, shaking regularly.

Strain through a muslin-lined sieve into a small saucepan. Add 2 teaspoons caster (superfine) sugar and stir over medium heat until the sugar has dissolved. Pour into a warm sterilised jar or bottle. Add 2-3 raspberries if desired, seal and label. Store in a cool, dark place for up to 6 months.

Spiced malt vinegar

SERVES 500 ML [17 FL OZ/2 CUPS]

Place 500 ml (17 fl oz/2 cups) malt vinegar in a saucepan. Add a 1 cm (½ inch) piece of fresh ginger cut into four pieces. Add 1 cinnamon stick, 2 teaspoons allspice berries, ⅓ teaspoon black peppercorns, 1 teaspoon brown mustard seeds, 10 whole cloves and warm over low heat. Pour into a warm sterilised jar and seal with a non-metallic lid. Stand in a warm place for 2 weeks. Put some peppercorns into a sterilised 500 ml (17 fl oz/2 cups) bottle. Strain and pour the vinegar into the bottle. Seal and store in a cool, dark place for up to 6 months.

Spicy apple and cinnamon vinegar

SERVES 500 ML [17 FL OZ/2 CUPS]

Combine 500 ml (17 fl oz/2 cups) white wine vinegar, 30 g (1 oz/⅓ cup) finely chopped dried apple slices, ¼ teaspoon black peppercorns, 2 bay leaves, ¼ teaspoon yellow mustard seeds, 2 cinnamon sticks, 2 sprigs thyme and 1 garlic clove in a 500 ml (17 fl oz/2 cups) sterilised jar or bottle. Seal and leave in a cool, dark place for 2 weeks. Strain the vinegar and pour into warm sterilised jars. Store in a cool, dark place for up to 6 months.

Tarragon vinegar

SERVES 500 ML [17 FL OZ/2 CUPS]

Warm 500 ml (17 fl oz/2 cups) white wine vinegar over low heat. Gently bruise 1 tablespoon fresh tarragon leaves in your hands and put in a 500 ml (17 fl oz/2 cups) sterilised wide-necked jar. Pour in the vinegar, seal with a non-metallic lid and shake well. Allow to stand in a warm place for weeks to infuse. Strain and return to the clean sterilised bottle. Add a sprig of tarragon, seal and label. Store in a cool, dark place for up to 6 months.

Index

Index

Published by Bay Books, an imprint of Murdoch Books Pty Limited.

Murdoch Books Australia
Pier 8/9, 23 Hickson Road
Millers Point NSW 2000
Phone: + 61 (0) 2 8220 2000
Fax: + 61 (0) 2 8220 2558
www.murdochbooks.com.au

Chief Executive: Juliet Rogers
Publishing Director: Kay Scarlett

Project manager: Paul O'Beirne
Editor: Vicky Fisher
Design concept: Heather Menzies
Design: Heather Menzies and Jacqueline Richards
Photographer: Natasha Milne
Stylist: Kate Brown
Food preparation: Christopher Tate and Grace Campbell
Introduction text: Leanne Kitchen
Production: Kita George

ISBN 978 0 681 53385 1

Printed by i-Book Printing Ltd. PRINTED IN CHINA.
This edition published 2008.

IMPORTANT: Those who might be at risk from the effects of salmonella poisoning (the elderly, pregnant women, young children and those suffering from immune deficiency diseases) should consult their doctor with any concerns about eating raw eggs.

CONVERSION GUIDE: You may find cooking times vary depending on the oven you are using. For fan-forced ovens, as a general rule, set the oven temperature to 20°C (35°F) lower than indicated in the recipe.

NUTRITION: The nutritional information given for each recipe does not include any accompaniments, such as rice or pasta, unless they are included in the ingredients list. The nutritional values are approximations and can be affected by biological and seasonal variations in foods, the unknown composition of some manufactured foods and uncertainty in the dietary database. Nutrient data given are derived primarily from the official NUTTAB95 database.